AI ASSISTANTS

The MIT Press Essential Knowledge series

A complete list of the titles in this series appears at the back of this book.

AI ASSISTANTS

ROBERTO PIERACCINI

The MIT Press | Cambridge, Massachusetts | London, England

The MIT Press would like to thank the anonymous peer reviewers who provided comments on drafts of this book. The generous work of academic experts is essential for establishing the authority and quality of our publications. We acknowledge with gratitude the contributions of these otherwise uncredited readers.

This book was set in Chaparral Pro by New Best-set Typesetters Ltd. Printed and bound in the United States of America.

Library of Congress Cataloging-in-Publication Data

Names: Pieraccini, Roberto, 1955- author.
Title: AI assistants / Roberto Pieraccini.
Description: Cambridge, Massachusetts : The MIT Press, [2021] | Series: The MIT Press essential knowledge series | Includes bibliographical references and index.
Identifiers: LCCN 2020035377 | ISBN 9780262542555 (paperback)
Subjects: LCSH: Intelligent personal assistants (Computer software)
Classification: LCC QA76.76.E95 P48 2021 | DDC 006.30285/436—dc23
LC record available at https://lccn.loc.gov/2020035377

10   9   8   7   6   5   4   3   2   1

Roberto: Hey Jibo, what do you do all day long?

Jibo robot: Algorithms . . . lots and lots of algorithms.

CONTENTS

SERIES FOREWORD

The MIT Press Essential Knowledge series offers accessible, concise, beautifully produced pocket-size books on topics of current interest. Written by leading thinkers, the books in this series deliver expert overviews of subjects that range from the cultural and the historical to the scientific and the technical.

In today's era of instant information gratification, we have ready access to opinions, rationalizations, and superficial descriptions. Much harder to come by is the foundational knowledge that informs a principled understanding of the world. Essential Knowledge books fill that need. Synthesizing specialized subject matter for nonspecialists and engaging critical topics through fundamentals, each of these compact volumes offers readers a point of access to complex ideas.

Have you talked to a machine lately? Even if you think you haven't, most likely your answer should be "yes." Maybe your internet connection stopped working and you called your service provider, but a "recorded" voice greeted you instead of a human agent, and asked what the reason for your call was. Or while driving your car you wanted to call your friend without risking a fine, or worse, an accident: you pushed a button on the wheel and simply said "call Peter," and the mobile phone in your pocket started dialing the right number. Or you pushed a button on your smartphone and asked what the weather would be like in the location where you were planning to spend the weekend. Or you asked the speaker in your living room to play your favorite music: "Hey Google [or Alexa, or Siri, or . . .]: Play smooth jazz." Or you talked to the remote control of your TV to search for your favorite show. Or. . . . In all of these situations you, willingly or not, spoke to a machine, or more likely to a computer either in the cloud, embedded in a device, or distributed between the cloud and the device. You did that to conveniently *do things*, like calling a friend, doing a web search, getting an answer to a question, setting an alarm, or being delighted by your favorite music or film. And in all of those situations, and many others like them, more likely than not you got the results you wanted. Doing so seemed quite easy and natural, since using speech to accomplish things is easy and natural for all of us, much more so than using a keyboard or a remote control device. In reality, underlying that ease of use and naturalness is a huge amount of technological complexity. Furthermore, unfortunately, applications of these technologies don't always work as well as we would like.

Each of the preceding scenarios involves a virtual assistant—the focus of this book. An *AI virtual assistant* is a machine made of a number of computer programs running on some remote server—but also, sometimes, embodied in specialized devices—that understands and responds to human voice commands. In the course of this book I will use the terms *AI*, *virtual*, and *AI virtual assistant* interchangeably. The technologies, the algorithms, and the programs making that possible required decades of technological and scientific research, and are by no means working to perfection, at least not yet.

This book offers the casual reader a high-level yet accessible overview of the principles and the technologies behind modern virtual assistants such as Apple's Siri, Amazon's Alexa, Samsung's Bixby, and Google Assistant. Some of these technologies required several decades of research, successes, and numerous failed attempts for virtual assistants to reach the capabilities they have today. And as we all know, much remains to be done to achieve the goal of a truly intelligent, reliable, and trustworthy

An AI virtual assistant is a machine made of a number of computer programs running on some remote server—but also, sometimes, embodied in specialized devices—that understands and responds to human voice commands.

automated assistant able to converse naturally with us. This book tries to provide an accessible account of those histories, and the motivations that created incentives for hundreds of scientists and technologists around the world to work on that, and for the commercial and academic institutions to fund those researches.

The desire to build machines that would produce and understand human voice goes a long way back in history. As we will see in the following chapters, attempts to mechanically synthesize human voice go back to the end of the eighteenth century, while the recognition of what is spoken started in the mid-1950s.

I clearly remember when as a young researcher in Torino, Italy, in the early 1980s, I happened to be in the audience at a convention where Marvin Minsky gave the keynote address. Minsky was a famous MIT professor considered to be one of the founding fathers of AI. I don't remember the precise words he used, but he said something like: "Intelligence is what computers cannot do yet. Today computers can prove theorems and play chess better than most human beings. But they cannot walk on two legs, or speak and understand speech like humans do. All of those things are easy and natural for humans, but still hard for computers. That's the real intelligence that computers have not mastered yet."

Indeed, back in the 1980s computers that could speak and understand speech were still in their infancy, and their

Some of these technologies required several decades of research, successes, and numerous failed attempts for virtual assistants to reach the capabilities they have today.

capabilities were quite far from what we experience today. We made strides in the past decades, and we do have impressive technologies that allow computers to understand a large variety of spoken languages and to speak back to us, their users, even though they are still far from humanlike capabilities. When the conditions are not perfect, owing to the presence of background noise, strong accented speech, or unusual questions asked in an uncharacteristic linguistic form, to give some examples, these automated virtual assistants do not come back with the right answer, or do not come back with an answer at all. However, even with today's imperfect technologies, large companies like Apple, Amazon, Samsung, and Google have enabled a significant portion of the world population to access the capabilities of these early virtual assistants. Not only is this true for the developed industrialized world, but also these technologies are being made available in developing countries to help people cope with lower levels of literacy and sparse availability of basic services.

This book is organized as follows:

In chapter 1, after a brief history of virtual assistants, I describe what the main components that enable spoken communication between humans and computers are and why building machines that understand spoken language is difficult.

In chapter 2 I provide a broad historical overview of AI and machine learning, with particular emphasis on the techniques used for building virtual assistants.

Chapter 3 is dedicated to speech recognition and to providing a detailed description of what the technological challenges are, how they were approached in the past, how they evolved, and how they are being approached now.

Chapter 4 describes the problems and the solutions around natural language understanding: in other words, the problem of going from a textual representation of speech to its meaning expressed in a symbolic form that can be used by a machine to provide an answer or perform an action.

Chapter 5 described the technologies that make a machine speak, from the generation of textual language to a speech signal.

Chapter 6 is dedicated to the dialog manager, the module that manages the conversation, the answers, and the actions performed by the assistant, and orchestrates all of that toward the fulfillment of user requests.

Chapter 7 is a discussion of the different way a machine can interact with humans. In particular, the chapter describes the emerging field of social assistants and robots.

Chapter 8 concludes the book with a look at the social impact of virtual assistants and discusses how they need to evolve in the future to increase their impact in our day-to-day lives.

WHAT IS A VIRTUAL ASSISTANT?

Although researchers around the world had been building machines that could understand speech and speak back on a number of simple tasks, the first AI (artificial intelligence) assistant introduced to a number of US users was Wildfire, a telephone assistant built by Wildfire Communications, a Boston-based company that was funded in 1992. Wildfire was responding to a number of specific user needs by combining the convenience of a customizable directory service with the functionality of an intelligent answering machine. Even though the product was not very successful from a commercial point of view, Wildfire demonstrated how a well-designed user interface could cope with the deficiencies of speech recognition programs' imperfect technology.[1] Motivated users would learn how to use a system with a pleasantly sleek, intelligently conceived user interface. Well-designed recorded prompts suggested the options one could choose from, while speech recognition could be conveniently constrained to recognize only those options. The profession of voice user interface (VUI) design started with Wildfire.

Energized by the idea that an intelligently crafted VUI could enable speech recognition use for narrowly scoped telephone applications, startup companies started to license technology from research institutions like MIT and the Stanford Research Institute (SRI). The startups then used these technologies to engineer platforms and applications, primarily for the customer service sector.[2] The soaring costs of employing human operators to provide fast assistance to their customers motivated companies to explore and adopt speech recognition–based customer care. Telephone virtual assistants—often referred to as virtual agents rather than assistants, since they provide a substitute for human customer care agents—also known as interactive voice response systems (IVRs) brought tangible benefits both for the companies deploying them, in terms of reduced customer care costs, and for the final user, in terms of readily available services. In many cases the reality was that virtual agents based on speech recognition actually provided a faster and often better service. Users seeking customer care did not have to stay in a telephone queue listening to music for a long time to finally get services from untrained agents with a poor mastery of the language. However, customers did not see that necessarily in the same way. It was annoying, to say the least, for someone seeking the solution to a problem to have to talk to a *dumb* computer, rather than a human agent. And it was also a reality that many systems were poorly designed, and the speech recognition capabilities were not exactly optimal, at least not for everyone, and especially not for people with accents or in poor acoustic conditions. However, despite the negative feedback of many customers interacting with virtual agents, speech technology continued to grow both at the industrial level and as an academic research topic.

Not much changed until 2011 when Apple launched Siri, the first smartphone-based virtual assistant as a feature of its new iPhone 4S. Siri was the product of a spinoff of the Stanford Research Institute (SRI) acquired by Apple a few years earlier. Siri was based primarily on the same speech recognition technology used by the customer-care telephone applications. However, voice did not travel on telephone lines; it was digitally encoded on the smartphone and sent, without any degradation, to the servers. But the main difference between Siri and the infamous IVRs was that the smartphone virtual assistant was not imposed on angry customers trying to solve a problem via an imperfect speech recognition system while navigating often badly designed menus. Instead, Siri was available as a product intended for interested users, who soon found that using it could also be fun.

At her first appearance Siri provided a number of basic services, including searching for local businesses, providing weather forecasts, and making phone calls. But one of Siri's most popular features was her personality, her witty answers to funny questions, her jokes. Word of mouth spread from one blog to the next and on social networks about what questions to ask Siri to get a fun response, such as "What's the meaning of life?" or "Where can I bury a body?" Thanks to the massive adoption of iPhones, Siri was potentially available to a large user base. That was the first time speech recognition, natural language understanding, and synthetic speech were introduced to—and not imposed on—millions of people. And of course the product benefited from this exposure, by getting constant improvements based on users' feedback and on the large amount of data gathered from iPhone users.

Following the success of Siri, and with analogous functionality, Microsoft announced Cortana in April 2014, a virtual assistant available for their operating systems and phones. Cortana relied on Microsoft's expertise in speech technology developed in years of advanced research in the field.

In September 2014 Apple enabled the "Hey Siri" feature. Users could now summon the virtual assistant with "Hey Siri" without having to push the home button on an iPhone or iPad. Only two months later Amazon announced Alexa and the Echo device.

Amazon's Alexa was the first virtual assistant with a dedicated device, a cylindrical speaker with only a couple of buttons to turn it on and off and make it stop listening. One of the most interesting features was the LED ring on top of the device. When a user activates the virtual assistant by saying "Alexa," the LED ring indicates the direction from which the voice is coming. This feature is a sign that Alexa is listening to a specific speaker, giving the device some sort of anthropomorphic behavior, such as when we turn our heads toward someone talking. The LED ring indicating the direction of the person calling Alexa was not intended as an ornamental feature, but also reflected the internal working of Alexa's audio processing. In fact, one of the problems in using Alexa and subsequent virtual assistant devices is that of far-field speech recognition. Voice collected from a distance includes more noise and reverberation than voice collected from a device closer to the mouth, like a smartphone. That noise and reverberation, caused by the sound bouncing on acoustically reflective surfaces like walls or windowpanes, would naturally degrade speech recognition accuracy. Knowing the direction from which the speech is coming, one could develop algorithms to attenuate the noise and reverberation coming from different directions. Alexa came with seven microphones, and used them for that purpose. The LED ring was a visualization of that process.

Sometime after Alexa was launched, Amazon announced a series of tools, including speech recognition, text-to-speech, and natural language understanding, available for third-party developers to build their own applications for Alexa, which were called *skills*.

Google Home came out in November 2016. At the same time Google made the assistant available on Android-based smartphones, and successively as an iPhone application. Google also launched Actions on Google, a set of tools to allow third-party developers to build Google Assistant applications. In response to Amazon Echo and Google Home, Apple shipped a Siri-activated speaker, called the Home-Pod, in 2017. Also in 2017 Samsung announced Bixby, its virtual assistant for the Galaxy smartphone.

Adding a screen to a virtual assistant was the next long-awaited advance. Amazon shipped its Echo Show in 2017, adding display and touch functionality to Alexa. Google then shipped several screen-based devices powered by the Google Assistant, and commercialized by third parties, such as Lenovo and JBL, as well as Google's Nest.

And there we are, with a number of virtual AI assistants available on phones and home devices, and soon rapidly available for other devices, such as watches and TVs, in homes, automobiles, and on the go. But how do those virtual assistants work and what are the technological issues related to them? The next section of this chapter will give a high-level view of the components that make a virtual assistant, while the following chapters will shed light on the deeper workings of those components.

What Makes a Virtual Assistant

An AI virtual assistant is not just a large piece of monolithic software, but rather, it is made of a number of components, each designed to resolve a specific challenge, such as recognizing, understanding, and producing speech. Each of these challenges has been a topic of technological research for several years, and most of them are still far from solutions that would compare with the analogous capabilities of humans.

In the broadest terms, a virtual assistant can be represented by the conceptual diagram of figure 1.

While each component, or module, of a virtual assistant and its related technology will be described in more detail in the following chapters, the following brief descriptions will familiarize readers with the terms used throughout the book (please refer to the glossary included in this book for the full list of terminology).

• The A/D (analog to digital) and D/A (digital to analog) converters are the entry and exit points from and to the analog world of audio signals and the digital world of computers. The A/D module transforms the audio,

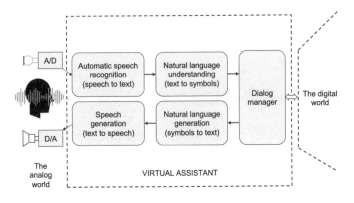

Figure 1 The architecture of a general virtual assistant.

and in particular the speech, collected by a microphone into sequences of numbers represented digitally in a computer form, mostly without any accuracy loss. In other words, any transformation made by the computer on those sequences of numbers can be thought of as transformation made on the input audio signal. The D/A converter performs the opposite function, and converts a sequence of numbers into analog audio signal. A/D and D/A converters are an established and pervasive technology that is used in any digital device where sound goes in and out.[3]

• Automatic speech recognition (ASR) transforms human speech into a textual representation of the words that were spoken.

- Natural language understanding (NLU) processes the sequence of words corresponding to the input utterance, and transforms it into a symbolic representation of its meaning. In practical terms, NLU converts text, which is meaningful to humans, into symbols that are meaningful to computer programs.

- Natural language generation (NLG) takes symbolic requests from the dialog manager and transforms them into meaningful sequences of words that will be spoken back to the user or shown on a display.

- Speech generation, commonly known as text-to-speech (TTS), transforms textual sequences of words into speech that humans can comprehend.

- Dialog manager (DM) takes the symbolic meaning of an utterance as input, and decides what the next action to perform is, also considering the whole history of the interaction and all contextual knowledge available. The dialog manager determination could be a request for the external digital world or for the NLG to generate something to speak back to the user.

- The digital world encompasses everything that can be queried or controlled digitally, external to the virtual assistant. That includes the accessible web, web search, and web answering; web services (such as weather forecasts, restaurant and flight reservations);

home automation via digitally controlled devices (such as light bulbs, appliances, door locks[4]); and anything else that is specifically built to interact with the virtual assistant.

As you can see from this list, speech and natural language technologies occupy an important—if not the most important—role in the development of a virtual assistant. However, we may argue that a virtual assistant does not simply understand and generate spoken language. In fact, we can think of a future generation of virtual assistants for which speech is only one of several communication channels. For instance, devices already exist that interact with the user by voice as well as touch displays.

While we discuss human–machine spoken language communication, it is important to understand the difference between the conversational capabilities of a virtual assistant, and the intelligence behind it. We can make machines good at communicating with humans by using human language, but that does not necessarily mean that the machine is intelligent and useful. On the contrary, there are machines that do not have any conversational capabilities, but their intelligence makes them extremely useful. Take for instance software packages that help people complete their tax returns. Tax rules are very complicated, they change every year, and it would require hours and hours of work for a nonexpert person to meet the tax return deadline. Indeed, tax return software packages, such as TurboTax, do not have any conversational capabilities. The interaction between humans and the complex software is achieved solely by checking boxes, selecting from drop-down menus, or clicking buttons. However, those software packages demonstrate highly skilled levels of intelligence and expertise in their domain.

We can also think of the opposite case, when machines can show conversational capabilities similar to humans, but with very little intelligence beyond that. The classic example is Eliza, one of the oldest chatbots built in the 1960s that simulates a session with a psychoanalyst.[5] During a short interaction with the chatbot, Eliza provides the illusion of understanding what you say and maintaining a seemingly intelligent conversation. But the illusion is short lived. After a few turns of interactions it is clear that Eliza is based on a simple pattern-matching and substitution method that can be implemented by a few lines of text processing code. Many other chatbots followed Eliza. The smartest ones have access to the wealth of data offered by the web, and they can carry on a seemingly intelligent conversation that is much like the casual chitchat you may have with a stranger at a party.[6] Of course such minor discourse is an important element of our social life, and a smart chatbot can fulfill that need. However it is important to understand that the chatbot's goal differs from that of a utility (or goal-oriented) assistant. A well-designed chatbot can be fun to talk to, but it may fail at accomplishing even simple tasks, like those a human assistant or a less chatty assistant would easily be able to fulfill, such as booking a hotel, or determining when the user needs to leave in order to beat the traffic and arrive for an appointment on time.

Then why is speech important for a virtual assistant? One of the most important reasons why we have spent decades trying to develop and build voice-based conversational machines is that natural spoken language is the easiest and most convenient way for a human to communicate with a machine. Imagine you are sitting at your dinner table and you want to know what the capital of Kazakhstan is, its population, and how far is it from your location. By using a home device, like Google Home or Echo, you don't even have to pull out your mobile phone or go to your computer. Simply ask your question in the same way you would ask a human, and your device will speak back to you with the right answer right away. In other situations, such as when you are driving or cooking at the stove, and you cannot push buttons on a touch display, speech is likely the only practical way to interact with the digital world.

Thus convenience is and always has been one of the main motivators for creating a spoken language interface to a virtual assistant. But there are other factors. Language allows us to express complex concepts that would

Natural spoken language is the easiest and the most convenient way for a human to communicate with a machine.

require a complex visual interface. For example, you can say something like "set up a reminder two hours before my next appointment with my dentist." Designing and implementing a graphical interface with buttons and drop-down menus with the capability of allowing these types of expressions where a concept (e.g., time for the reminder to be set) is defined by another concept (e.g., two hours before my next appointment) is quite hard if not impossible. This is the compositional nature of language, and we could extend it arbitrarily. For example:

Set up a reminder two hours before the second appointment with my dentist this week.

Set up a reminder two hours before my second appointment with the person I met today at 10 am.

Set up a reminder to give me enough time to drive to the next appointment with the person I met this morning at 10 am.

Compositionality is the power of language, and humans are good at understanding complex queries. Today's virtual assistants can emulate this to a certain limited extent, but once we can build these capabilities in a robust manner in a virtual assistant, the advantage of spoken language communications with machines will be even more evident.

Let's conclude this chapter with some considerations about the inherent complexity of spoken language communication.

Why Spoken Language Communication with Machines Is Hard

Spoken language is as natural and easy for us as walking, recognizing the faces of people we know, or finding our way home from work. We learned our mother tongue during the first years of our lives, and it is so natural to us that we never think about the complexity hidden in spoken language. But if you ever try to learn a second language as an adult, you may realize all of a sudden that speaking and understanding are not as easy as you thought. You have to focus consciously on the rules of grammar and syntax of the new language, strain to recall words you've memorized, and articulate them using sounds that are alien to your ears. And you have to put words together in a way that may be different from that prescribed by your mother tongue. Would adjectives go in front of nouns, or the other way around? What's the gender of the word *table*? How do you construct an irregular verb and make it work with adverbs, or auxiliaries? However difficult this learning process may be, learning a new language gives you only a glimpse of the complexity of this wonderful invention of the human brain that gave us the evolutionary advantage to become what we are and to change the world, for better and for worse.

The complexity of spoken language is huge.[7] As a matter of fact, we still have a lot of open questions on how our brain generates and decodes languages, how it produces and understands speech, and how it can manage abstract concepts, like love and beauty. In practical terms we know very little about what happens beyond the mechanics of our speech and auditory organs. We know that speech is produced by the flow of air through our larynx, which may result in either a periodic (e.g., in a vowel sound) or noise-like (e.g., in a consonant sound like /f/) signal that is then modulated by the shape of our vocal tract characterized by the different positions of our tongue, lips, and velum. But then, it is still largely a mystery how the brain generates the nerve signals that activate our articulatory muscles simply starting from an idea or a concept in our mind to eventually produce understandable spoken words. Similarly, we know that the vibration of the air caused by other people's speech is propagated through the eardrum to the middle ear and then to the inner ear's cochlea that converts it into an electric signal that travels to the brain through the auditory nerve. We also know what the auditory nerve signals look like, but how those signals become words and concepts in our mind likewise is still largely a mystery.

We still have a lot of open questions on how our brain generates and decodes languages, how it produces and understands speech, and how it can manage abstract concepts, like love and beauty.

To be fair, many of our hypotheses on how the brain may produce and process language are mostly based on experimental evidence. However, we do not have a clear step-by-step procedure, or better an algorithm, that would enable a machine to produce and understand human languages as well as we do. Since what the brain does is mostly inscrutable, for hundreds of years linguists and cognitive scientists have been studying human languages from a phenomenological point of view, and then speculating about the inner workings of the brain. Most theories about the human language describe it based on a number of layers of abstraction known as phonetics, morphology, lexicon, syntax, and semantics. We are not saying that the human brain uses those abstractions, but they are a good way to explain linguistic phenomena and describe language from a scientific point of view. In the early times of speech and language technology, researchers tried to replicate those theories as a set of rules, often arranged into similar layers of abstraction, with the goal of creating computer programs able to speak and understand speech. Even though some of these theories proved useful to create a foundation for the current technologies, we realized that a different approach, often referred to as the engineering or brute force approach, worked best.

Until very recently, the engineering approach drawn from advanced computer science and mathematical constructs continued to improve the performance of most of the modules described by figure 1, as we will see in the following chapters. However, a new paradigm has emerged that does not require building complex programs, but rather allows for machines to be built that can learn from examples. This approach is known as *machine learning*, and in particular its latest evolution, called *deep learning*, has allowed us to build systems that can derive a symbolic understanding of complex patterns, such as speech and images, with performance nearing and sometimes even surpassing that of humans. Deep learning has improved the speech understanding and generation capabilities of machines tremendously, and it is relentlessly making the transition from research to industry.

AI AND MACHINE LEARNING

Now let's take a detour and talk about AI, or artificial intelligence, in general and not limited to its application in building a virtual assistant. In fact, to understand most of the components of figure 1 used in today's virtual assistants, it is important to acquire a basic understanding of what AI is and its evolution toward the most recent technology known as deep learning.

If we were to trace the history of artificial intelligence from its beginnings to the present, we could identify a number of distinct paradigms. However, as happens usually in technology, each new paradigm did not immediately displace what preceded it, rather, the different schools of thought often coexisted for some time, until it was clear to everyone that the new methods were far superior than the old ones.

Classic AI, the first paradigm to consider, takes us back to the summer of 1956, when the term *artificial intelligence* was used for the first time at a workshop held at Dartmouth College in Hanover, New Hampshire. John McCarthy, the organizer, invited scientists who were or would later become known as the pioneers of what today is called *computer science* in general and *AI* in particular. Claude Shannon, Herbert Simon, Marvin Minsky, and others worked together for nearly two months to understand how to "make machines use language, form abstractions and concepts, solve kinds of problems now reserved for humans, and improve themselves."[1] After the workshop the AI pioneers and their acolytes continued to discuss and develop their ideas about making computers play chess or logically prove theorems.[2]

Classic AI was characterized by rule-based systems. Scientists wrote the rules in excruciating detail with the help of domain experts. The rule repository was the *knowledge base* used by the system to perform logical reasoning. When confronted with a problem to solve in the domain of the knowledge base, an *inference engine* applied the rules in a recursive manner until a solution was found, or the system ran out of rules. For example, if the domain was blood infections like those represented in the early expert system called MYCIN, the input data would be the specific results of a blood test performed on a patient.[3] Some of the MYCIN knowledge base rules might apply to those test results, triggered by values that were above or below a certain threshold. Each triggered rule produced hypotheses that would recursively trigger other rules, in a process called the *inference chain*, until a solution or a final hypothesis was found. During the application of rules, the inference engine may have found different plausible competing hypotheses that were scored using heuristic techniques, which were generally defined by the same experts who created the rules. In fact, some of these systems were also called *expert systems*, because their goal was to emulate the experts who crafted the rules and heuristics.

At that time there were many systems built following the architecture of MYCIN. Although each of those systems may have had different ways to do inference and to apply heuristics, the basic idea was essentially the same: a combination of rules and heuristics following a series of logical steps to solve complex problems. The researchers' task was to find the best and most representative way to code rules, the most effective heuristics to evaluate competing hypotheses, and the most efficient inference engines.

Automatic speech recognition and understanding were not immune from the charm of the expert system paradigm proposed by classic AI. Using the same approach as MYCIN, many labs built complex systems of rules that would start by recognizing the individual sounds in a speech signal, then compose them into words, sentences, and finally a symbolic representation of the meaning. The rules created for those systems ranged from specific acoustic phenomena (e.g., If the silence before a burst of speech energy is between 10 and 30 msec long then the sound is that of a stop consonant), to morphological and lexical phenomena (e.g., if the word *you* is followed by the word *all* then the final /u/ of the first word and the initial /a/ may be merged into a single neutral vowel, as in /y'all/). Syntactic and semantic rules were also included in the knowledge base to rule out ungrammatical and non-meaningful hypotheses and to determine what the actual meaning of the input sentence was. Of course, in order to write all those rules, the research labs had to enlist acousticians, phonologists, lexicographers, syntacticians, and semanticists to cover all the levels of abstraction of human language, and software engineers to write the programs that would put all of that together.

The *expert system approach* to speech understanding attracted the interest of many scientists. Rationalizing and describing, as rules, a large amount of knowledge that was not readily available in a computerized form seemed to be a good way to advance and validate a theory of language. However, the main reason for using rules created by experts was the hope that the behavior of the final system could be explained in a rational manner. By looking at the applied chain of rules, scientists could understand the decisions made by the system, and eventually correct them in case of malfunction. Large multidisciplinary teams of experts in fields as varied as engineering, linguistics, and psychology were collaborating to solve the difficult but compelling problem of developing machines that could understand speech.

Unfortunately, none of those systems painstakingly built with considerable effort by several experts in the field ever achieved results that led to their deployment for practical applications. As we discussed earlier, one of the reasons for the failure of expert-based speech-understanding systems lies in the intrinsic variability of speech and language that defy any characterization by rules. Writing a complete set of rules to identify the fundamental speech sounds of a language, the words, and eventually the meaning based on the acoustic evidence of an utterance is practically impossible without making errors. Those errors cannot be corrected without writing more rules and exceptions to those rules, in a process that does not scale and thus produces inherently inaccurate systems. Knowledge-based speech recognition research survived until the mid-1980s, when it became clear that a purely engineering-based method exemplified by data-driven template or statistical speech recognition was poised to outperform them.

Machine Learning

Machine learning, often simply called ML, is the general evolution of classic AI that abstracts from the need to code all the possible rules that presumably characterize a phenomenon to be recognized or predicted. ML systems are based on a learning engine, often referred to as an *agent*, that can learn from a large collection of examples, called the *training set* (or *training corpus*, or *training data)*, that is as representative as possible of the phenomenon we want to characterize. The three major categories of machine learning are: *supervised*, *unsupervised*, and *reinforcement* learning.

The term *supervised* in supervised learning refers to the fact that each example in the training set is associated with a label that represents its true identity, which is exactly what we want the engine to be able to detect in unlabeled data. The learning engine's job is to make an association between the training data and the labels, and to generalize its learning by automatically labeling any new piece of data that is not part of the training set. For instance, the training set for a machine learning–based speech recognizer would consist of a large set of utterances and the correct identity of the words spoken in each of them. Once trained, the speech recognizer would be able to correctly identify the words in any arbitrary utterance that has not been part of the training set.

Conversely, in *unsupervised* learning the training set does not have labels. We ask the engine to learn what labels would best apply to that set, and successively to be able to characterize any arbitrary piece of data with one of

Machine learning is the general evolution of classic AI that abstracts from the need to code all the possible rules that presumably characterize a phenomenon to be recognized or predicted.

those labels. As you can imagine that is a much harder task, even for humans. Imagine giving a large set of recorded utterances to someone in a language she doesn't know, with the task of learning the words of that language in order to recognize them in any segment of speech of that language she hears in the future. The problem is quite complex, also considering there might be no pauses between words. If the training set is large and varied, she would notice that similar sequences appear in different contexts, and that could be a clue to help her identify different words. However, that may be complicated by the fact that different words in different contexts, in that particular unknown language, may have different morphology, and thus sound slightly different.

The task of learning in an unsupervised manner is familiar to anyone who has worked to decrypt ancient languages, for example, hieroglyphs.[4] The task seems nearly impossible. An automated approach to unsupervised learning, called *clustering*, consists in grouping individual pieces of data into a number of groups, or clusters. All the pieces of data in a cluster have a higher degree of similarity than those belonging to different clusters. Automated clustering can detect repeated units that could be associated to the words of that language. Unsupervised learning is the holy grail for speech recognition, since without the need to manually transcribe training speech, a speech recognizer could learn from arbitrarily large amounts of training data, and keep learning while it processes new data. Scientists are making tremendous progress in unsupervised learning for speech recognition to reduce the need to transcribe speech data and improve speech recognition accuracy.[5]

While supervised and unsupervised machine learning systems are based on a training set, reinforcement learning requires the active participation of the agent in the task we want it to learn. For a given task, the learning engine starts by trying to accomplish it with some initial built-in knowledge. Any time the agent does something that brings the machine closer to the completion of the assigned task (most likely by chance at the beginning), it receives a *reinforcement* signal in the form of a positive numeric reward. When the agent does something wrong it may receive negative feedback in the form of a negative numeric reward, or cost. The job of the agent is to tune its strategy, also called *policy*, to accumulate the largest amount of rewards. Let's go back to our example of a person trying to learn an unfamiliar language without knowing a single word of it, but having access to some fluent speakers of that language, although these individuals do not have any other language in common with the learner. One strategy that the learner may apply is to *try* some simple communications after she has been exposed to some new words of the language. For instance she could try pointing at objects while speaking a random word of the unknown language she has heard before, and wait for the fluent speakers to approve with a smile or disapprove with a frown. Eventually, after many attempts, she might say the right word and get a smile. A systematic way to implement that strategy would be for her to *explore* as many possible unknown words by pointing at numerous different objects, while trying to receive as many smiles as she can. While exploring new words, the learner can also try to *exploit* the words she has already learned to confirm what she knows. The tension between exploration and exploitation is one of the issues addressed by different reinforcement learning algorithms.

As we saw we are not ready to use unsupervised learning for problems like speech recognition and natural language understanding. Likewise, the use of reinforcement learning for virtual AI assistants is still a topic of academic research.[6] However, some limited form of reinforcement learning has been used for virtual assistants, as we will see in chapter 6's discussion of dialog management.

Statistical Machine Learning

The term *statistical machine learning*, also called *statistical learning*, refers to computer programs that learn how to classify or predict phenomena based on statistics extracted from training data. Let's consider an example. Imagine you want to predict automatically whether a particular

Reinforcement learning requires the active participation of the agent in the task we want it to learn.

song is going to be liked or disliked by people based only on their age. The first thing you need to do is collect supervised data. In this extremely simple example you have only two labels: like and not-like. Then you select a number of subjects with a significant representation of the age demographics of your audience, and ask each subject whether they like or do not like the song. If you collect a significant number of samples, you have a labeled training data set. Each piece of data in your data set consists of two values: the age of the subject and the label indicating whether the subject liked or not-liked the song. This is a supervised data set, in which the subject's age is a free variable, and the like/not-like label is the supervision. With this data you can analyze the distribution of ages—presumably different—for the likes and the not-likes. Depending on the song you choose for your experiment you may find a significant difference between the age distribution of the two labels. For instance, you may find that the likes are roughly distributed as a bell-shaped curve, with the highest number of likes clustering around age 22. You may find that the not-likes are similarly distributed with their highest number concentrated around age 44. The two curves intersect at the age 35, meaning that an equal number of 35-year-old subjects liked and not-liked that song. An extremely simple statistical predictor of the likes/not-likes of your chosen song is whether the age of a person is below or above age 35. If below 35, most likely the person liked the song; if above 35, most likely that person did not. If your statistics truly reflect the real distribution of the population, your prediction will be right more times than wrong. How often will you be more right than wrong? Well, that depends on how good your statistics are; in other words, how many data points you have collected, how well your subjects statistically represent the actual population of listeners, and how effective a predictor age is for liking that song. Most likely you will make a lot of errors. You can make an estimate of your errors by taking a new data set, totally independent from your training data, often called a *test set*, and measuring how many people above age 35 like the song, and how many below 35 do not.[7]

However, using only age as a predictor of whether listeners like the song or not may not be accurate. Introducing more variables is a way to reduce the errors. Those variables could consider, for example, listeners' familiarity with that particular genre of music, measured by how many songs belonging to that genre they know, how many years of music education they have had, the size of the city of town where they live, their birth month, gender, education background, their systolic and diastolic blood pressure averages, the average summer and winter temperatures of the location where they live—and anything else you may think of. Now the problem of creating a machine learning statistical predictor with more than one variable is definitely more complex. Moreover, some of the variables can be numeric, such as listener age, and some may be symbolic, such as gender. In general, for each training data point corresponding to a listener, we have a supervision (a like/not-like label), and a set of values, called *features,* corresponding to all the variables we used to characterize each listener. The job of a statistical machine learning–based predictor, or classifier, is finding a function that, given the values of the features of a new listener, will predict whether they like the song or not. When we considered only one value, the listener's age, that *classification* function was very simple—whether the listener was younger or older than a certain age. Now the function may be more complicated and require more sophisticated calculation.

Establishing a general mathematical form that the classification function may assume, for instance a linear or higher order equation, or something more complex than that, is the job of a machine learning expert, and can be based on some assumptions or intuitions about the problem at hand. Machine learning methods that assume a specific form of the classification function are called *parametric*, since the goal becomes to learn the parameters of that function by using the training data set. There are many established parametric methods in statistical learning, such as logistic regression, Bayesian modeling, and linear discriminant analysis. Those methods have been well known and used for many years.

The other category of statistical learning methods where no assumptions are made on the nature of the data is called *nonparametric*. These algorithms include k-nearest neighbor, support vector machines, and regression-decision trees. Neural networks, and their modern deep learning evolution, are a special case of nonparametric learning, as we will see in the sections that follow.

Artificial Neural Networks

Parametric statistical machine learning has been effectively used for decades to address problems not only like speech recognition, natural language understanding, and text-to-speech, but also computer vision, resource optimization, and many others. However, one of the problems with parametric statistical machine learning is that its performance is generally bound by the limitations of the underlying model (e.g., HMMs, Bayes, higher order classifiers) in representing the phenomenon to classify, predict, or recognize. In practice, when we select a parametric model for statistical machine learning, we make a large number of simplifying assumptions, and the model does not completely match the underlying reality of the data.[8] Thus, while it is true that by increasing the amount of training data we would increase the predictive and recognition performance of the models, there is a point when they start to flatten to the point of diminishing returns. Instead, artificial neural networks, and particularly deep learning, are not tied to a specific parametric model or any underlying assumption, and by adding more data and increasing the size of the network, there is a good chance to see the performance increase.

Artificial neural networks, often referred to as *neural networks*, or just NNs, have been known for a long time as a nonparametric alternative to statistical machine learning.[9] The basic element behind neural networks is the artificial neuron: a simple computational element that takes a number of numeric inputs, multiplies each of them for a specific weight parameter, adds them up, and filters the final number with a nonlinear function. For example, if the resulting number is less than a defined minimum value, the output is set to 0 and if it is above a defined maximum value, the result is set to 1. See figure 2 for a more detailed description of the computation performed by an artificial neuron.

Each neuron has its own set of weights, one for each input, and different from neuron to neuron. Those weights are very important, as we will see. Of course, with a single artificial neuron we can do very little. However, if we put many of them together, by connecting the output of some to the input of others, we can do interesting things, like building classifiers and predictors, or approximating any arbitrary function.

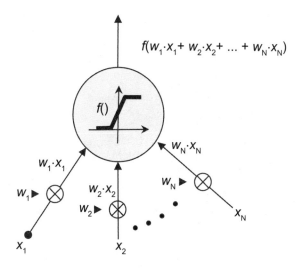

$$f(w_1 \cdot x_1 + w_2 \cdot x_2 + \ldots + w_N \cdot x_N)$$

Figure 2 Typical function of an artificial neuron. All input values x_1 to x_N are multiplied by their corresponding weights w_1 to w_N and added up. The sum is then filtered by a nonlinear function $f()$ resulting into the output value that may be passed on as input to other artificial neurons. The weights w_1 to w_N are learned by applying the backpropagation algorithm on a number of training examples.

Feed forward is one of the earliest and most popular NN architectures. In this type of NN an arbitrary large number of neurons are structured in layers such that some of them receive the input signals, that is, the *input neurons* belonging to the *input layer*, while some others, the *output neurons* in the *output layer*, send out their output—in other words, the final classification or recognition result. All the others, the *hidden neurons* in the *hidden layers* receive input

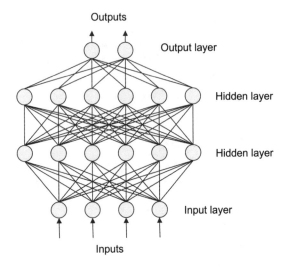

Outputs

Output layer

Hidden layer

Hidden layer

Input layer

Inputs

Figure 3   In a feed-forward multilayer, also called a deep neural network (or DNN), the neurons are arranged in successive layers, going from the input, through the hidden, and to the output layers. The output of each neuron feeds the input of the neurons of the successive layers. The input neurons receive the input values, and the output values represent the result.

and send output from and to other neurons of the adjacent layers (see figure 3).

It has been shown that at least three layers—an input layer, a hidden layer, and an output layer—are needed for a NN to approach an arbitrary classification or prediction problem.[10]

The weights of each neuron are the parameters that enable learning. An algorithm discovered in the 1980s and called *backpropagation* allows us to estimate the weight for the network to approximate an arbitrary function by using a number of supervised training samples.[11]

The backpropagation algorithm goes through each training example by using each training sample as input, making all the calculations, and obtaining output values that should correspond to the supervision value for that sample. The difference between the supervision label—what we would like the NN to generate—and the actual output for that sample is *propagated back*, and all the weights are modified in order to reduce the discrepancy.

Let's now go through a concrete and simple example of a neural network classifier. Imagine we have a black-and-white picture, for instance an image made of 64 × 64 = 4,096 pixels. Let's assume that each of those pixels can either be black and represented by the number 1 or white and represented by the number 0.[12]

Next, let's assume that we are looking only at images of individual digits written by hand. We would like to write a program that guesses, with the highest possible accuracy, which one of the ten digits is represented by the image. You can try to write a classic program with if-then-else rules, but that's nearly impossible. Then you can try using statistical machine learning. For instance, you can take a lot of examples of images of digits, and calculate the statistics for each pixel position in each one of the digits. That will not work very well, because digits can be written in many different ways, they can be written at an angle, small or large, and may not be centered in the 64 × 64 pixels image. So, if you are a skilled engineer, you may try to *normalize* the image. You can program transformations that make every image of a handwritten digit straight, centered, and pretty much of the same size. Then, since you understand the nature of handwritten digits, you will create a program to extract telltale features from your images. For instance, you can try to detect straight or curved segments, vertical, horizontal, or at an angle. This is what is called *feature extraction*. Notice that the features are defined by the programmer's knowledge of the problem at hand. Once you have defined the features, you can describe every image as a combination of them. Then you can apply some higher-level statistical model to the features extracted from each image and calculate, based on your training set, the probability that a combination of features represents a specific digit. You will probably find out that 1s have a high probability to be written with one or two straight lines, one of them at an angle and connected to the vertical one; and 9s have straight or curved lines connected to a closed circle on the top. That would work, to a certain extent, as long as the normalization and feature extraction are done properly. But of course the accuracy would depend on how well the normalization works, how insensitive the features are to the intrinsic variability of handwritten digits, and how well your statistical model fits the nature of the problem. And if you are not satisfied with the results, you can use more training data. However, your performance will eventually flatten out, unless you find better features and better statistical models. In other words, to develop a statistical machine learning classifier, you need to understand what the important features are for the problem you are considering, and what the best model is to represent that problem.

Neural networks are a simpler way to learn how to recognize the digits that in principle do not require the developer to make any assumptions about the features and the model representing them. For the same handwritten digit problem we saw earlier, we can use a regular feedforward network similar to that in figure 4. The input layer will need to have 4,096 neurons, one for each individual pixel of the image. The output layer will need to have ten neurons, one for each of the ten digits. For the sake of this example we will add just one hidden layer made of 100 neurons. The choice of the number of hidden neurons is arbitrary, but it affects the final performance. For each image, each of the 4,096 input neurons will receive a 0 or a 1, depending on whether the corresponding pixel of the image is white or black. Each input neuron will send its 0s or 1s to every one of the 100 hidden neurons that will do their computation as described by figure 3. Notice that each hidden neuron will receive 4,096 0s or 1s, will multiply each one by the corresponding weight—that would require 4,096 weights for each individual hidden neuron, so 409,600 in total—then sum all of that up, filter the resulting number with the nonlinear function, and output a number between 0 and 1. Each one of the ten output neurons, in turn, will get 100 numbers (one for each of the hidden neurons), perform the neuron computation, and get an output result. If the network has been trained properly, chances are that the output neuron corresponding to the correct digit represented by the input image returns a number close to 1, while all the others return a number close to 0. If that does not happen, during training, all the weights of the hidden and output neurons will be adjusted to get as close as possible to that situation, using the backpropagation algorithm, for each training sample. None of this requires any work by the developers to define feature and statistical models. In a way, it works like magic. That's the attractiveness of neural networks.

After the backpropagation algorithm gained popularity at the end of the 1980s, a growing number of researchers started to apply it to a large variety of problems, mostly classification and pattern recognition, with different degrees of success. However, for most of the problems, NNs did not appear to be superior to other methods based on statistical machine learning such as *Hidden Markov Models* (HMMs), the mathematical abstractions developed by IBM scientists to represent the statistics of the sequence of feature vectors of an utterance.[13] These had played an important role in speech recognition. It seemed that more training data and larger networks with more layers would lead to better results, but there were a number of problems with that. First, large amounts of examples for the most interesting problems were not readily available, and even if they were, the computers of the time were not powerful enough to handle immensely large training sets. Second, adding more layers, even if desirable, was not a viable solution back then. Scientists did not know how to train large networks with multiple hidden layers, mostly due to computational and intrinsic learning issues.

Another problem that contributed to the lack of popularity of NNs at that time was the sequential nature of many of the important research problems, such as speech recognition, natural language understanding, and *machine translation*. In fact, for all of those problems the inputs and outputs are sequences of features, symbols, or words, of arbitrary length. Unfortunately, the simple feed-forward neural networks we discussed earlier have a fixed number of inputs and return a fixed number of outputs.

However, these early neural networks were still used successfully for the recognition of patterns of fixed size, such as handwritten characters, or to model functions without any a priori assumption on their shape. For instance, some labs used them as a front end to a speech recognizer, to create a mapping between the input features of the speech signal in a short time interval, and the probability of each of the basic sounds for that interval. That mapping was then used by classic parametric statistical models to search for the most likely sequence of words.

We would need to wait nearly three decades from the popularization of the backpropagation algorithm in the 1980s to find an effective use of neural networks that would revolutionize the scientific and technological world.

Deep Neural Networks

The method of adding multiple hidden layers to improve the prediction and classification performance of neural networks has been known since the 1980s. However, the lack of availability of massive amounts of training data, the limited computing power available, and the consequent inferior performance when compared to other methods contributed to a loss of research interest in the topic. It wasn't until 2006—when a number of papers published by Yann LeCun, Yoshua Bengio, and Geoffrey Hinton and their teams at NYU and the Universities of Montreal and Toronto, respectively—revived the interest in deep neural networks with large numbers of hidden layers, typically between ten and twenty.[14] By contrast, networks before then typically had only one hidden layer. Networks with many layers started to be called *deep neural networks*, or

DNNs, and the learning associated with them was called *deep learning*.

The increased computational power, especially brought by the introduction of GPUs (graphics processing units) in commercial computers, allowed easy programming of massively parallel calculations, and fostered the application of DNNs in notoriously difficult challenges such as speech recognition. A number of publications appeared around 2009 in which DNNs were shown to work remarkably well for speech recognition. Around 2012, all major speech research labs started to use DNNs and showed unprecedented results on challenging speech recognition benchmarks.[15]

Initially, DNNs were used for speech recognition to replace the feature extraction process. Finding the right features for classic HMM-based speech recognizers had been one of the main problems that had engaged the research community for many years. In fact, finding features that would be insensitive both to the intrinsic variability of the speech signal and the acoustic variability of the environment had always been, traditionally, the seemingly unreachable holy grail of ASR research. Since the early days of speech recognition research, and before the advent of DNNs, researchers experimented with all sorts of transformations that would prove to be more robust to all types of variability, but only to a certain extent.

A transformation of the filter-bank features, called Mel-frequency cepstral coefficients (MFCC), and further transformations that the scientists had found in years of research and experimentation had been somewhat effective for increasing the performance of pure statistically based speech recognizers. However, feature extraction remained a topic of research among speech scientists, yielding additional transformations to render the features more insensitive to all sources of variability, and produce modest improvement on speech recognition accuracy. As a result, the front end of speech recognition systems became extremely complex and sophisticated. Only specialized speech and signal-processing engineers could create a front end that would guarantee the state-of-the-art recognition accuracy.

Since non-deep neural networks became popular in the 1990s, there have been attempts to use them as a front end to a speech recognition system. The idea was to train a neural network to transform a set of basic filter-bank features from one frame of speech, or from a small number of adjacent frames, into a vector that would represent the probability of that frame being a part of a certain phoneme. These attempts had some initial limited success. However, when the major speech recognition labs started to apply DNNs to the same problem, all of them realized unprecedented accuracy results on standard test sets that were known to be among the hardest tasks for speech recognizers. Those results convinced the scientific community of the advantages of using DNNs as a front end to classic HMM-based ASRs. Labs did not need to experiment with complex feature transformation and normalization with the hope of finding invariants. More data, increasingly larger neural networks, and faster computers would make the accuracy improve to levels never seen before.

One way to look at multilayered neural networks that may intuitively explain their success is that of successive layers of feature extraction. Imagine a DNN learning to recognize handwritten digits from images. Once properly trained, the first layer is able to learn to detect simple, basic features such as straight or curved strokes; the second layer learns to combine those features to discover more complex ones, such as strokes connecting at different angles; the third layer learns to detect even more complex features such as closed or open shapes, and so on. Each layer results in features from the previous layer being combined into more complex ones, so as the output layer can make an informed decision. Notice that in a pre-DNN era, all those basic and combined features, and the related algorithms, were determined by the engineers who developed the systems and were based on their intuitions of the specific classification problem.

Substituting the standard feature extraction module with DNNs was the beginning of the deep learning era for speech recognition. However, speech recognizers still included sequential modeling that required HMMs, and the need to search for the optimal sequence of models that would best match, in a probabilistic sense, the sequence of input feature vectors that were now an approximation of the probability of phonemes. Unfortunately, standard deep neural networks are not equipped to easily handle arbitrarily long sequences of input feature vectors and output symbols, such as the sequence of words resulting from the recognition of an utterance. A different architecture of neural networks was needed for that task.

Recurrent Neural Networks

Regular neural networks have a fixed number of neurons that receive input from a static pattern, for instance one or more feature vectors corresponding to a small portion of an utterance, or the pixels of a static image. Recurrent neural networks instead allow input patterns that develop along a time dimension and have a variable number of inputs and outputs.

To understand how recurrent neural networks (RNNs) work, imagine you feed a regular neural network input layer the features corresponding to a first small portion (called a *frame*) of an utterance in order to obtain the output values. Next you save the output values of each hidden neuron for that particular frame. Then you process the second frame with the same network and you feed the saved values to each corresponding hidden neuron, along with the regular values coming from the previous layer in the network. Then you do the same with the third frame, and so on, until you exhaust all the frames of the utterance. In practical terms, the contribution of each frame is combined with the result of the contribution of the previous frames. The results you get while processing the last frame thus include the contributions of each preceding frame.

Another way to look at a recurrent neural network is to observe it unfolded over time. Each input frame is applied to a copy of the network that gets signals coming from the copy of the same network that processed the previous frame. You can use this recurrent procedure both for training and recognition. The backpropagation algorithm can be applied to the unfolded network in a way that is analogous to that of a regular static network.

A modern architecture of a recurrent neural network is based on the encoder/decoder structure. The encoder is a regular recursive NN that processes the inputs. The final hidden values of the encoder, sometimes called *thought vectors,* are given as input to another NN that acts as a decoder. Finally, in a modern version, all the hidden values at each step of the decoder are weighted by another network, called the *attention network*, which learns how to put more emphasis on different parts of the input that are more relevant for the result.

One of the problems of standard RNNs is that for long sequences the information at the beginning of the sequence may be lost by the time the network reaches the end. For instance, regular RNNs may have a hard time translating from or to languages that have long-distance dependencies, such as German, Dutch, and to a certain extent English. Long short-term memory networks (LSTMs) are special types of recurrent neural networks that try to address the problem of long-term memory loss. LSTMs have internal neural structures, called *gates*, which can learn what information is important to carry over across a whole sequence and what information can be forgotten.

Another powerful evolution of DNNs is the convolutional neural network (CNN), where the operations performed at different layers are referred to as convolutions. Convolution is a mathematical operation that involves the point-by-point multiplication of two multidimensional signals—for example, different patches of an image or different segments of an audio signal. CNNs have been applied to image processing and recognition, producing exceptionally good results.

As we have seen, there are different architectures of recurrent neural networks depending on the characteristics of the problem and the latest theoretical results that continue to produce better and better architectures. In any case the size of these networks is massive, including millions of connections and corresponding weights, thus requiring special computational architectures, including special processors. As we will see in the following chapters, DNNs are rapidly changing all the technologies used for virtual assistants, starting from speech recognition, to natural language understanding, language generation, and dialog management. Now that you have an idea of the different methods that fall under the rubric of *machine learning*, it is time to go back to our virtual assistant and look at each one of the components of figure 1 in more detail.

SPEECH RECOGNITION

Most likely you have heard about automatic speech recognition, or ASR, many times in the past, and hopefully experienced it as a positive evolution of technology. However, chances are that if you have been exposed to ASR, voluntarily or not, you may have been frustrated, annoyed, or perhaps amused by its mistakes. It is a fact that speech recognition has not been working that well until recently, at least not always, and not for everyone. Indeed, today ASR's effectiveness greatly surpasses that of only a few years ago, thanks to the incredibly large amounts of data available to train it, much more powerful computers, and, as we will see, deep learning. However, even though some labs claim that ASR surpasses human performance in tasks such as transcribing conversations, there are many situations where it is still inferior to human capabilities, such as in a highly noisy and reverberating environment;

when many people speak at the same time; in the presence of highly accented speech; or when people switch among different languages in the same utterance.[1] Humans can communicate effectively even in these challenging circumstances, but machines still have issues.

The goal of speech recognition is to identify the words that were spoken in an utterance with the highest possible accuracy. In other words, speech recognition is expected to do what a typist would do. A typist puts on paper exactly the words that were spoken, but he is not required to understand the meaning of what he types. Of course, a good typist must be proficient in the language he is typing and have a certain level of understanding of its grammatical rules, and to a certain extent some understanding of the meaning of what he hears. That is important for improving accuracy and avoiding mistakes due to ambiguities—for example confusing the words *read* with *red,* or *four* with *for,* or by transcribing, out of context, "recognize speech" as "wreck a nice beach." Likewise, a good ASR needs to have some notion of how words are put together and follow each other in the language it is trying to recognize in order to reduce the chance of mistakes. Understanding their meaning is not its job, but some level of understanding could help. But again, like a typist, the ASR's job is merely to transcribe what it hears—nothing more than that. Yet that alone is not a simple feat. It took more than sixty years of research in many labs and universities around the world to accomplish what we have today: good ASR but not perfect, or at least not consistently as accurate as humans.

The dream of building a universal ASR that could transcribe any arbitrary utterance in any specific language has been around since the beginning of the digital era, and even before that, challenging researchers and technologists for decades. Besides the scientific challenge, academic and industrial researchers were motivated by a number of interesting applications that they could build once ASR reached reasonable levels of accuracy, even for simple cases like strings of digits or commands that do not require deep understanding of the utterance's meaning. In the era of the speech recognition pioneers, the second half of the twentieth century, industrial research speculated about applications such as automated telephone dialing, controlling machinery with voice commands, and getting weather or flight information via the telephone. It would take many decades before these simple tasks would actually be deployed.

The very first speech recognizer we know of was built in the 1950s. That was the work of three Bell Laboratories scientists, K. Davis, R. Biddulph, and S. Balashek, who implemented a clever procedure on analogic hardware to recognize sequences of digits separated by short pauses.[2] The machine, as big as a room and full of vacuum tubes, resistors, and capacitors, had to be tuned for each particular

The goal of speech recognition is to identify the words that were spoken in an utterance with the highest possible accuracy.

speaker in order to achieve the best performance. Remember that digital computers did not exist before 1945, and even in the early 1950s were expensive, rare, and excruciatingly slow. Everyone thought they were good only for performing lots of abstract calculations, and not for interpreting signals coming from the real world, such as speech.

It was only in the 1960s, and mainly in the United States and Japan, that research labs started to consider the use of digital computers to process speech and language. The invention of A/D and D/A converters made that possible by allowing analog electric signals—such as audio captured by a microphone—to be converted into a sequence of numbers, then processed digitally and transformed back into an audio signal.

The use of computers for processing speech and language fostered research in all areas of human–machine spoken communication, including speech recognition and speech synthesis. Labs around the world started investing in large-scale human–machine spoken interaction research, but the results were generally quite disappointing, to the point that a prominent institution like Bell Laboratories banned any work on ASR, at least for a while.[3] ARPA, the Advanced Research Projects Agency of the US Department of Defense, resurrected the dream of talking machines by starting a large project known as SUR (Speech Recognition and Understanding) in 1970 with a considerable amount of funds directed to the major academic and industrial research labs, such as MIT, Carnegie Mellon University, Bolt Beranek and Newman (BBN), and SRI, the Stanford Research Institute.[4] The goal of the project was to build machines that could converse naturally with humans about a defined domain.

At that time there were two schools of thought and two corresponding approaches to speech recognition. One of them was the expert system approach, also known as the *artificial intelligence*, *rule-based*, *knowledge-based*, or *rationalist* approach.[5] The other was the *engineering approach*, often dubbed the *brute force* or *empirical* approach. The expert system approach followed the AI principles of the time—in other words, trying to emulate human reasoning (or at least what they believed we knew about it) as closely as possible. An expert system was a general method for building reasoning systems based on large sets of rules handcrafted by experts in the field, and used by an inference mechanism with the goal of embodying, in the machine, the knowledge applied by the experts themselves. For instance, expert linguists in areas as diverse as phonetics, lexical morphology, syntax, and semantics, could craft a large number of rules to progress from the most elemental sounds to the meaning of sentences.

However, there were at least two problems with the expert system approach. One was that it could not scale.

In order to get better and better performance, or to extend the system to new domains, many new rules had to be added. That required a lot of manual labor by experts who would continue to add rules to account for exceptions, but would never reach a point when the rules covered all the possible situations. The second problem was that in reality human language is not totally governed by strict rules. From the perception of sounds to the semantic understanding of a sentence, strict rules may cover around 80 percent of the situations in language use, but the remaining 20 percent are exceptions to the rules. Language cannot be hard-coded as rules; it is mostly a *fuzzy* phenomenon. Any hard-coded rule can, and will, make mistakes sometimes, and the accumulation of errors would necessarily lead to poor performance.

Indeed, the majority of the labs that accepted the challenge of the ARPA SUR project followed the expert system approach and failed to achieve an acceptable performance at the end of the five-year project. Only one system, HARPY, built by Raj Reddy's team at Carnegie Mellon University, based on a brute-force engineering approach, demonstrated performances that were superior to all of the other systems, and very close to the SUR project requirements.[6]

HARPY was the only system in the ARPA SUR competition that deviated from the classical rule-based expert system approach of the time. The basic principle of HARPY was that of *templates*, snippets of sample speech sounds coded and stored in a training phase to then be used to measure their similarity with corresponding segments of the incoming speech to be recognized. The templates were arranged as a graph. Any arbitrary path on that graph represented a legal query for the chosen domain.[7] Speech recognition was then reduced to the problem of finding a path in the graph that had the most accumulated similarity to the utterance to be recognized. Isolating and preparing the templates during the training phase required some manual work, but since the number of fundamental sounds of a language is finite and not very large, and their combination can represent all the words of a language, the approach was easily scalable to any set of words, and any number of domain utterances. The definition of a similarity metric between the stored templates and segments of the incoming speech made the recognition problem analogous to searching for the lowest-cost path in a graph. Well-known optimization techniques could easily solve that problem. With the computers available at that time the recognition of an utterance required several minutes of computation.

However, with far better speech understanding capabilities than those of all the other AI-based systems, HARPY definitely demonstrated that the brute force approach had the potential to be superior to any other rule-based approach.

The Template Approach

As shown by HARPY, a brute force/engineering approach to speech recognition was more promising than the classic and elegant expert system approach.[8] Toward the end of the 1970s, several labs in the United States and Japan developed better template-extraction and matching techniques for very specific and simpler tasks than those called for in the ARPA SUR project. For instance, the recognition of strings of digits could be performed with reasonable accuracy with templates of whole words and a matching technique called *dynamic time warping* (DTW).[9] DTW took into consideration the nonlinear time expansion and contraction that are typical of different utterances of the same word, even from the same speaker. The word *eight*, for example, can be spoken at a slower or faster tempo. However, the expansion or compression rates for different parts of the same word can be different. As an example, while we can arbitrarily expand or compress the duration of a vowel (say *a . . . aa . . . aaaaa*), we cannot do the same with certain consonants (try to make a longer or shorter /t/ sound). So, matching an arbitrarily longer or shorter word with a stored template of the same word had to account for some portions of the word that might be more stretched or compressed than others. DTW was the solution to that.

Of course, even though DTW was very successful, many problems remained. First of all, matching arbitrary utterances with a set of templates still required the automatic identification of the beginning and end of each individual word in a stream of audio coming out of a microphone. The only way to approach that, at that time, was to force the speaker to insert pauses between consecutive words. That used to be called *isolated speech recognition*. Pauses are relatively easy to identify in a stream of audio. Simple thresholding techniques, known as end-point detectors, based on heuristic logic applied to the energy of the signal worked quite well, unless in the presence of significant background noise. Furthermore, some scientists figured out how to extend the DTW algorithm in order to search for the best sequence of words, even though the beginning and end of each word were not identified by pauses, in what was called *connected* (or *continuous*) speech.[10]

The other problem with templates is that they represent instances of words uttered by a particular speaker. So, if a different speaker attempted to use a speech recognizer trained with templates that were not her own, the recognition accuracy would degrade significantly. For that reason those early systems were called *speaker dependent,* since each speaker had to train the system before using it by going to the process of recording each word of the vocabulary. That problem could be alleviated by collecting templates for a large number of people with the aim to statistically represent the entire population of potential speakers. Of course, the more templates used, the better the chances to represent a larger population of speakers, and thus get better performance for anyone. But using a large number of templates increased the computational demand posed on the slow computers of the time to a point that it was not possible to accomplish speech recognition in real time. Some researchers tried to compress the number of templates into a smaller number by selecting the more representative ones based on a technique called *clustering*, but the *speaker independence* accuracy of the template method never achieved a satisfactory performance.

The collection and preparation of word templates remained a labor-intensive process. Every time a new word was added to the vocabulary to be recognized, or a new vocabulary was to be adopted for a new system, someone had to collect new templates from all the potential speakers. HARPY had demonstrated that one could successfully build templates of basic speech sound elements (like phonemes, or groups of phonemes), and concatenate them to create templates for any possible word. But it was not easy to extract those subword templates efficiently without a lot of manual labor, or automatically with a reasonable accuracy.

However, the template-based approach enabled some limited commercial applications of speech recognition for small vocabularies (some dozens of words), and available to a limited number of speakers. Unfortunately, slightly more sophisticated applications were a challenge for early

ASR systems for the reasons discussed previously: the isolated speech requirement, lack of speaker independence, and the laborious process to collect templates for any new words added to the system. Their accuracy was also not good enough to support a large-scale deployment for applications that would prove useful for a large portion of the population. Ambient or telephone line noise, speaker and speaking style variability and strongly accented speech contributed to the difficulty of making speech recognition practical.

Fortunately, despite a long series of unsuccessful attempts, the goal of developing accurate speech recognition systems to enable virtual assistants and many other applications remained alive and well for a number of industrial and academic institutions around the world. Only in the mid-1990s did we see a number of applications begin to expose ASR to a potentially large number of users. These applications were in the areas of dictation and telephone-based customer care, and they used a totally new, principled methodology based on statistics.

Automated Typewriters

From the 1930s until the advent of personal computers and word processors, electric typewriters were one of the main product lines of IBM. By removing the need for a human to push keys on a keyboard, a totally automated voice-driven typewriter was indeed a long-term vision for the business machines giant. The prestigious Thomas J. Watson Research Center located in Yorktown Heights, New York, was the home of a group of scientists who had been pursuing that vision since the 1960s. But it was not until the 1980s that Fred Jelinek, the head of the IBM speech recognition research team, finally unveiled the technology that would power speech recognizers around the world for decades, until quite recently. The technology was not based on the imitation of humans, nor on the use of linguistic rules, nor even on the manual collection of templates. It was based on a novel *data-driven* approach that today would fall into the machine learning category.

Fred Jelinek was known to have said, "Every time I fire a linguist, the performance of our speech recognition system goes up," to stress the fact that the best speech recognition performances were obtained by automated, *knowledge-agnostic*, data-driven methods, meaning that there was no need to explicitly code the knowledge that linguists have about language into a program.[11] In fact, the IBM group, since the late 1970s, started to look at the problem of transcribing words automatically from speech as a telecommunication problem. They cast the speech recognition problem as that of designing an optimal receiver that tries to detect the original message—the identity of the words in an utterance—in the presence of noise, represented by the intrinsic (e.g., caused by humans speaking differently every time) and environmental (e.g., caused by ambient noise) variability of the speech signal. Their solution relied on the definition of a statistical model for calculating the probability that a speech signal—or better yet, a compressed and discrete digital version of it known as "acoustic feature vectors"—would correspond to a specific sequence of words. Under this paradigm, solving the speech recognition problem was then equivalent to solving the following two problems:

1. **Training:** estimating a reliable statistical model that would take a sequence of acoustic feature vectors corresponding to an utterance and calculate the probability of that sequence representing a specific sequence of words.

2. **Search:** given a sequence of acoustic feature vectors corresponding to an arbitrary unknown utterance, and a trained statistical model, finding the sequence of words with the highest probability of having generated the corresponding speech signal.

It turned out that the statistical models for calculating the probability of a sequence of words given a sequence of acoustic feature vectors extracted from an utterance can be thought of as two distinct components. The first is the *acoustic model* that represents words in terms of acoustic features vectors in a statistical manner. The second component is the *language model* that represents the different probabilities associated with different sequences of words. In other words, the language model represents the fact that the sequence of words "animal wild lion is the a" has a much lower probability of being spoken in the English language than the sequence "the lion is a wild animal."

We will discuss the statistical models for speech recognition in more detail later. For now it is important to realize that this approach represented a big departure from the rule-based approaches of the AI systems and was in a way an evolution of the labor-intensive template-based approach. Rather than defining rules based on the knowledge that linguists had accumulated about speech and language, the IBM scientists, mostly engineers and mathematicians, used a purely knowledge-agnostic statistical perspective. That was what powered the brute force approach. The HMMs are based on an extension of the theory of the Russian mathematician Andrey Markov. Fred Jelinek and Jim Baker—part of the same team at IBM— developed the HMM approach based on the work carried out by Leonard Baum at the Institute for Defense Analysis at Princeton.[12] That approach would empower the speech recognition engines until close to the present day.

While HMMs described the statistical relationships between words of a language and the speech signal represented as sequences of feature vectors, the language model described the probabilistic properties of any possible sequence of words. The basic elements of a language model were modeled as probabilities of short sequences of two or three words, called *n-grams*. The "n" in n-grams refers to the span of words that are modeled acoustically. If that span is three words, they are called *trigrams*. For instance a trigram may specify that after having observed the sequence of words *want to*, the word *sue* is generally, in common language, highly more probable than the word *spaghetti* and slightly less probable than the word *go*. Of course the probabilities of words depend on the specific domain of language upon which they have been calculated. It may happen that for a particular domain, say that of legal correspondence, the sequence *want to sue* is slightly more probable than *want to go*, but both of them are far more probable than *want to spaghetti*.

Both acoustic models and language models need to be *learned* (*trained*, or *estimated*) based on a large number of training utterances and a large amount of text, respectively, generally called a training corpus. The larger the amount of data, the higher the performance of the resulting system, because the statistical models are more representative of the general acoustic and linguistic phenomena in spite of the variability introduced by the different speakers, noise, environmental acoustic conditions and the many ways to express the same concept that are available in a language.

In 1997 both IBM and Dragon Systems shipped software products that could run on PCs and allowed users to dictate letters or reports. Both competing products, respectively called ViaVoice and Naturally Speaking, were initially quite limited. The size of the vocabulary—the number of words that the speech recognition software could recognize—was limited to a few thousands, the software programs required the users to speak a few hundred utterances to allow the systems to adapt to their voices, and their speed and accuracy were far from optimal. However, ViaVoice and Naturally Speaking turned out to be commercially successful in a number of niche markets, like those of radiologists and lawyers who were used to dictating reports and letters, and now could use computers instead—much cheaper than hiring a typist. The ability to adapt the dictation software to a specific domain and to the voice of a specific user allowed the systems to deliver reasonable performance that guaranteed their usability. Successive versions of the two products included new features and better accuracy, but they always catered to small markets. Despite the fact that a few years later Microsoft and Apple both included the speech recognition software as part of their operating systems at no additional cost, dictation software never achieved a widespread popularity.

Automated Telephone Agents

The 1990s had witnessed the rise of interactive voice response (IVR) systems that allowed users to interact with remote applications by pushing buttons on a telephone. Some of those applications are still responding to a variety of toll-free numbers. Who has never called a company such as a bank, insurance, or a service provider and had to deal with an often unwieldy sequence of recorded menus instructing the caller to "press one for this, press two for that"?

IVR systems were introduced when push-button telephone pads started to replace the old rotary dials on telephones. The new dialing technology was known as DTMF (dual-tone multi-frequency signalling) and is still available on older landline phones. Systems installed at the telephone exchanges could detect in a straightforward and accurate manner which buttons the caller pushed. In fact each button on the telephone keypad corresponds to the transmission of two distinct tones at different frequencies. Simple circuits detect the two frequencies and unequivocally determine which button, or dial number, the caller pushed.

The idea of DTMF-based IVR technology was to enable a caller to control a remote automated system by pushing one or more numbers on the keypad, while the user was clearly instructed on which number to push by a recorded voice prompt. That would allow the automation of simple services that traditionally were executed by human operators.

Initially the IVR systems were quite simple, and allowed users to choose from a small number of options, such as which type of service a user wanted. In fact AT&T, which at that time had a monopoly on long-distance US telephone service, installed one of those systems for customers to allow them to choose which type of call they wanted to make. The service offered only five options— using a calling card, making a collect call, charging to a third party, reaching a specific person (person-to-person), or making an operator-assisted call—and after choosing, the call was completed accordingly or relayed to a human operator. Unfortunately a large number of phones in the country, and especially payphones, still had the old rotary dial that did not work with the DTMF IVR system. That's how the idea of using speech recognition came about. By instructing the caller to speak the words corresponding to which of the five services they desired, AT&T could extend the automated service to all phones, including the old rotary ones. That system was called *voice recognition call processing*, or VRCP.

Although the job of the speech recognizer in the system was quite simple, that is, recognizing one of the five words/phrases, (i.e., calling card, collect, third-party, person-to-person, operator), issues such as noise on the line, truncated utterances by callers speaking too early or too late, and the variety of accents of the caller population required the invention of new technologies to allow the ASR to reach the required level of accuracy. Bell Laboratories, the research branch of AT&T, developed a number of new solutions that helped overcome those issues.

The system was successfully deployed in 1992, and it is said to have saved AT&T hundreds of millions of dollars every year. It also created some public controversy, with rumors and suggestions that AT&T would lay off a number of operators after the deployment of the system.[13] Indeed, the main motivation to develop IVRs, either touch-tone or voice based, was to save money, especially on services that did not generate revenue. The cost of installation and maintenance of an IVR system was much lower than paying a staff of human agents, also considering the need to train the agents.

Encouraged by the success of AT&T's VRCP and the evolution of speech recognition thanks to the statistical model approach, the transformation of touch-tone IVR into voice IVR became very popular in the mid-1990s and is still in effect today.

The main limitation of touch-tone automated telephone systems is that there are only ten possible choices, equal to the number of buttons on the keypad. In order to build complex applications, the solution was to offer hierarchical choices through a number of successive menus, or to ask the caller to push a number of buttons in sequence.

For instance, for flight information services, the DTMF systems typically asked to push the buttons corresponding to the first three letters of the departure or arrival city as consecutive button presses. Indeed, the first three letters would allow you to unambiguously select some of the cities, but produced ambiguous results for many others. For instance the three buttons corresponding to NEW are the same for New York, New Orleans, Newark, New Haven, and other locations. Thus, a DTMF IVR needed to ask the caller one or more questions to disambiguate the departure or arrival city, such "push 1 for New York, push 2 for New Orleans," and so on. Of course, using voice solved the problem by allowing the caller to just speak the full name of the city. However, needing to recognize large lists of words raised a number of technological problems, especially considering that confusion among similar sounding words in a large list is far from rare.

Speech recognition systems of the time were designed to recognize only a limited number of words or phrases that developers had to define using a *speech recognition grammar* for each step of the interaction. We will discuss grammars in more detail in chapter 4, but for now think of a grammar as an efficient and compact way to list a large, possibly infinite number of potential phrases and their related meanings.[14]

Given that at any point in time during an interaction the ASR could recognize only a limited number of words and phrases as defined by a grammar, the prompts had to be designed to solicit responses that would match those words and phrases, and reduce the chances for users to say something unexpected that would either not be recognized or be confused with another option. Open prompts, such as "Please tell me the reason you are calling," had to be avoided in favor of more explicit instructions on what to say, such as "Please say account balance, transfer between accounts, or pay bills." This was the case until the early 2000s, when new technologies began to emerge that allow callers to make more open responses to prompts.

So prompts and grammars can be seen as the two faces of the same coin. On the one hand, prompts instruct the user on what to say; on the other hand, grammars are designed to recognize exactly what the prompts suggest. This is called *directed dialog*, as opposed to *open dialog*, in which users are not explicitly prompted on what to say at a specific turn of the interaction. In directed dialog interactions, if a prompt is changed, the corresponding grammar needs to be revised accordingly. The design of the system responses and of the overall structure of the dialog is an art mastered by voice user interface (or VUI) designers, a new breed of professionals who started after the introduction of the IVR systems and specialized in designing the virtual agents and virtual assistant interactions.[15]

In the late 1990s, the business of building voice-based IVR created an ecosystem of companies and specialized

The design of the system responses and of the overall structure of the dialog is an art mastered by voice user interface (or VUI) designers, a new breed of professionals specialized in designing the virtual agents and virtual assistant interactions.

professions. For instance, companies like SpeechWorks and Nuance provided speech recognition software and professional services, while companies like Cisco and Dialogic provided platforms that allowed speech recognition to interact with the telephone network. Other, smaller companies provided VUI design consulting services.

In 1999 a consortium including AT&T, Lucent, IBM, and Motorola proposed a computer language, called *VoiceXML*, to standardize the development of audio and voice response applications, such as IVRs. W3C (the World Wide Web Consortium) took ownership of VoiceXML and extended it to become a mainstream industrial standard. VoiceXML was based on the notion of a voice browser, analogous for speech to a regular web browser.[16] When the user inputs a URL in a web browser, such as Chrome or Safari, or clicks a button on a web page, such as SUBMIT or SEARCH, the browser sends a request message to a server via a protocol called *HyperText Transfer Protocol* (HTTP). The invoked server sends back, to the very same browser, a document, in other words a file, with text, images, videos, or sounds. That file is formatted according to a language called *HyperText Markup Language* (HTML) that instructs your computer how to show text and images and how to play videos and sounds. A voice browser, however, does not run on a personal computer but instead runs on a remote server connected to the telephone network. When a user calls a specific number (a 1–800 customer care number, for example) the voice browser sends an HTTP request to an application server for that particular service, which in turns sends back a document coded in VoiceXML to the voice browser. The VoiceXML document instructs the voice browser to play a prompt and start a speech recognition process with certain parameters and a specific grammar. As the user speaks and the speech recognizer transforms that speech into text, the voice browser sends that transcription back to the application server. The application server, based on the speech transcription, decides which VoiceXML document to send to the voice browser next, and so on. The logic governing which VoiceXML document to send back to the voice browser is one example of what we call a dialog manager, the subject of chapter 6.

Voice XML could also handle simple form-filling dialogs through an algorithm known as FIA (form interpretation algorithm) that allowed users to speak a number of fields (such as origin, departure, date, and time for the identification of a flight) in any combination and order, in what was called *mixed-initiative dialog*.

The introduction of VoiceXML made the process of developing a telephone speech application analogous to developing a web application, thus leveraging the experience of web developers. A number of companies started hosting VoiceXML browsers that could be used by third parties who would pay for their usage to run speech recognition–based applications. TellMe, later acquired by Microsoft, was one of the first companies to provide VoiceXML pay service to speech recognition–based application providers.

Google launched GOOG-411 in 2007, a toll-free telephone directory assistant that was one of its first successful voice recognition applications. Although it was still aimed at landline telephone users, it paved the way to the next revolution: speech on the internet.

Internet Speech2Text

With the advent and mass adoption of always-online smartphones, the idea of using the internet—as opposed to the telephone line—as the transport channel for speech in ASR applications was considered a natural evolution. In the mid-1990s, Mike Phillips, a speech recognition pioneer, cofounded SpeechWorks, one of the first companies to develop core technology for speech IVR. In 2006, Phillips went on to cofound Vlingo with John Nguyen. The idea behind Vlingo was to enable smartphone services that would send digital speech through the internet and get a response back on the mobile phone either spoken or displayed as text or images. At about the same time, another company, funded by Igor Jaboklov, a former IBM employee, launched a similar service called Yap. Vlingo eventually was acquired by Nuance, and Yap by Amazon.

Sending speech through the internet has several advantages. First and foremost, the quality of the signal reaching the speech recognizer is not limited by the telephone lines. Regular telephones transmit speech with a 4 kHz bandwidth, the minimum frequency for intelligible speech. Indeed, some of the sounds with high frequency components can still be confused for one another, such as /f/ with /s/ or /b/ with /v/. Expressions like "V as in Victor," "F as in Frank" are often necessary to disambiguate between similar sounds, simply because of the limited bandwidth of the telephone lines. Digitized speech sent via the internet can easily use higher bandwidth, for instance 8 kHz, with a reduced confusion among similar sounds and better speech recognition accuracy. Besides the limited bandwidth, the other problem with telephone lines is the line noise. On regular telephone lines, for those who remember them, callers occasionally experienced background noise and echo that affected speech communication. There is practically no noise added to speech during a digital transmission. Speech is digitized at the source, sent as packets of numbers on the internet, and received pretty much unaltered at the end. Ambient noise, for instance, can also be mitigated by smartphones by using noise-cancellation microphones, and the implementation, on the smartphone itself, of noise reduction algorithms.

Thus there were only advantages derived from using speech on the internet. The only problem was that internet coverage, at that time, was not always guaranteed, and the cellular internet was not always fast enough for transmitting speech, therefore introducing noise by the loss of packets, and latency of the response. But those were transitional problems, since the cellular networks were constantly increasing their coverage and speed.

Thus the idea of hosting speech recognizers in the cloud to process speech transmitted digitally over the internet, often called *Speech2Text* services, started to gain momentum in the industry. Major companies that had been involved in speech recognition research early on, such as IBM, AT&T, and Microsoft, started offering cloud-based speech recognition. Leveraging their initial speech experience with GOOG-411, Google started offering cloud-based Speech2Text services. In 2011 Google launched Google Voice Search. Desktop and cellphone users could click on the microphone icon on the Google search box and speak their query to see the search results virtually right away.

Leveraging internet-based speech recognition, another revolution was soon to come: virtual assistants on smartphones. Siri Inc, a small spinoff of SRI, the Stanford Research Institute, made a standalone virtual assistant application, also called Siri, available at the iPhone App Store some time before Apple acquired the company and launched Siri as an integral feature of its iPhone 4S in October 2011. That was the start of the virtual assistant era.

But let's look now at how modern *traditional* speech recognition works, before delving into the topic of advanced neural end-to-end models. Pretty much until today, industrial grade ASRs have been thriving on statistical parametric modeling, in particular Hidden Markov Models. While advanced research is moving into neural end-to-end models, many of the HMM-based speech recognizers are still used. Understanding how a statistical ASR works provides a basis for comprehending the complexity behind the problem of speech recognition, and the leap forward recently achieved by deep neural networks.

Statistical Parametric Speech Recognition

Figure 4 shows the architecture of a classical statistical speech recognition system. This type of system is still in use today although, as we will see, many of the modules are being replaced by more modern machine learning based on neural networks. Indeed, in order to understand the complexity underlying the process of recognizing speech, it is important to look at the classic architecture as described by figure 4.

The next sections of this chapter will discuss the functionality of all of the modules shown in figure 4.

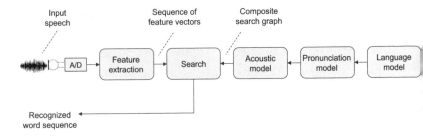

Recognized ←
word sequence

Figure 4   Block diagram of a classic speech recognizer.

Feature Extraction

As shown in figure 4, input speech is collected by a microphone. and the electric signal is digitized by an A/D converter in order to be processed by a computer. The resulting digital waveform is too variable and has too many insignificant details to provide a suitable representation for statistical models. Consider, as an analogy, the task of characterizing the geography of a country: you don't examine each grain of sand or stones, but instead you look at significant features such as coasts, mountains, and borders with other countries. Since the early era of speech recognition, it was clearly necessary to use a more compressed and significant representation obtained by extracting a number of features that characterize the speech signal at regular intervals of time.

Speech is a dynamic phenomenon, a signal that is continuously changing its characteristics. When we speak, the organs that produce speech, typically called the *vocal tract*—the lips, tongue, larynx, vocal chords, and velum connecting the mouth cavity with the nose—are always in continuous movement. There is never a stationary moment, since the articulatory muscles activated by the brain to control each tiny movement of the vocal tract are always moving from one configuration that produces one sound, to another configuration that produces the next sound. For instance, when you speak the word *pot* your vocal tract starts from a configuration where the lips touch each other to block the airflow for a fraction of a second. Immediately after that the lips open suddenly to release the burst of acoustic energy that is characteristic of the /p/ sound.[7] But that happens while the vocal tract is already moving toward a round-lipped configuration for the pronunciation of the vowel /o/, while at the same time the tongue forms a hump toward the posterior part of the mouth cavity, and the larynx starts vibrating to produce the periodic sounds that characterize vowels like /o/. But even before the configuration of the vocal tract reaches the configuration for the /o/ sound, it is already moving toward that for the next sound /t/, which is produced by blocking the airflow with the tongue touching the ridge behind the teeth on the roof of the mouth, then opening the blockage and releasing the air immediately.[18] And of course, while pronouncing the final /t/, the articulatory muscles are already preparing to move toward the first sound of the next word. That's how we produce a word through continuous articulation, with our vocal tract always in motion, never still.

However, the organs that produce speech do not move at an infinite speed. It takes a finite amount of time for the lips to close, the tongue to move, the larynx to start vibrating, or the velum to lift to let the air pass through the nose and produce sounds like /n/ and /m/.[19] Scientists who started to work on the processing of speech many years ago already determined that 10 msec (milliseconds), one hundredth of a second, is a time interval short enough to consider the movement of the articulatory organs quite insignificant, and long enough to be able to characterize the speech signal in terms of its spectral characteristics, or distribution of frequencies. So, with a good degree of accuracy, we can consider speech as a sequence of stationary intervals of 10 msec each, called *frames*, that can be characterized by their spectral content.

A common way to characterize the spectral content of a frame of speech is to measure the amount of energy allocated in different frequency intervals, or bands, typically a dozen or so, that are spaced along the frequencies to replicate the resolution of the human ear, known as the "Mel scale."[20] By doing so, a frame can be characterized by a dozen or so numbers representing the energy in each one of those frequency bands. You can imagine how *sibilant* sounds like /s/ may have more energy at high frequency components than sounds like /v/, and how vowels like /a/

or /u/ have a harmonic structure that distinguishes them, much like the sounds coming from different instruments such as a clarinet or a trumpet. This representation is also called a *filter bank*. Later, speech scientists found out that they could apply some transformations to those numbers and add other information to improve the performance of their ASR.[21] Eventually the standard representation of a frame of speech became a few dozen numbers for every frame of 10 msec, called a *feature vector*.

The feature vector representation was known and used even before the advent of more sophisticated statistical machine learning. Templates of words, or of phonetic units, popular in the 1970s as we saw earlier in this chapter, were also represented as sequences of feature vectors of this type. Thus a frame could be considered as a point in a multidimensional space, where each number of the feature vector represents one of the coordinates of that point. The template-matching algorithm, the dynamic time warping or DTW algorithm, used metrics, not dissimilar to the Euclidean distance between two points in a multidimensional space, to compare each individual frame of a template with each one of the incoming speech and find the best possible match, that is, the one with the minimal cumulative distance between the sequence of input frames and each template. Indeed, template matching can be considered to be one of the first rudimentary data-driven machine learning approaches to speech recognition, where templates constituted the training data.

When Hidden Markov Models were introduced by the IBM scientists, they offered a more principled, statistically based approach that abstracted from the need to define a heuristic frame-by-frame distance metric. HMMs provided a statistical framework designed to optimize a well-defined overall optimality criterion that was somewhat related to the minimization of the amount of recognition errors.

Acoustic Model
Hidden Markov Models are parametric probabilistic models that, once trained, can be used to calculate the probability of any arbitrary sequence of feature vectors. Since HMMs are parametric models, training means estimating their parameters based on a corpus of training data, or, in other words, a large number of utterances labeled with the sequence of words that were spoken. If, after training, one were to calculate the probability of a speech segment from the same training set with their corresponding HMM, let's say the probability of a segment corresponding to the word *one* calculated using a trained HMM for the word *one*, that probability likely would be higher than the probability calculated with the same model for a different segment, let's say the word *two*. Of course, nothing can be said for a segment of speech that was not in the training set, but if

the training corpus was large enough, the probability of a segment corresponding to the word *one* from speech that was not in the training set would still be higher when calculated with a trained model of the word *one*. Keep in mind that by using HMMs one could train models for each defined speech segment—words, syllables, or phonemes—from a large speech corpus without having to segment that speech into the corresponding units.

Thus one could train an HMM for each word in the vocabulary and use them to recognize any arbitrary sequence of those spoken words. However, if new words were to be added to the speech recognizer, one would have to train a model for each word. That is not practical. Rather, if we build HMMs of elemental speech sounds, like phonemes, we can compose them to synthesize models for any possible word or phrase. In US English, for example, there are roughly forty phonemes. Thus forty trained HMMs could be composed to form models for any possible US English word. However, a system with only forty HMMs, one for each phoneme, will not be very accurate because the acoustic characteristics of the phonemes are strongly influenced by the phonetic context in which they are pronounced. As we discussed earlier, speech sounds are highly dynamic. When the vocal tract is producing one sound, it is already moving on a trajectory to be ready to produce the next sound. Because of that, the spectral characteristics of each sound are highly influenced by the previous and following sounds. This phenomenon, known as *coarticulation*, affects all sounds that compose an utterance, including those at the boundaries of words. This phenomenon is even stronger in certain languages including US English, where phonemes can often disappear at the junction of words, for example: /you all/ can easily become /y'all/.

Because of the phenomenon of coarticulation, simply building an HMM for each phoneme won't be an accurate model of that phenomenon in different contexts. A solution used in modern speech recognizers employs an HMM for each phoneme in any different phonetic context. Thus, for each phoneme p of a language, we need an HMM for each x_p_y, where x and y are all the possible phonemes that could appear before and after p respectively, including preceding and trailing silence. How many HMMs do we need to properly represent any utterance in a language that has N phonemes? In general, we need $N*N*N$. For English, with N roughly equal to 40, we need $40 \times 40 \times 40$ = 64,000 HMMs. Even though not all sequences of phonemes are possible, that's roughly the required order of magnitude for the number of acoustic models. The set of trained HMMs corresponding to all the defined phonetic units is called the *acoustic model*. As we stated before, an acoustic model allows us to calculate the probability of the corresponding phonetic unit for any possible, and arbitrary, sequence of feature vectors.

HMMs are complex models that require the estimation of a large number of parameters. It is not uncommon for a high-performance system to require hundreds, if not thousands of parameters for each HMM. For example, for a 1,000-parameter HMM, we would need to estimate $64,000 \times 1,000 = 64$ million parameters to get a full set of models. In practice, scientists found ways to reduce that number to a more reasonable size, especially when large amounts of training data were not available. In any case, the order of magnitude of these numbers—the number of models and the number of parameters—gives you an idea of why large amounts of training data are essential. Typically, to get proper models for speech recognition, the training set consists of millions of utterances. And even that amount may not be enough. In fact, the speech recognition mantra has always been: "There is no data like more data."

Pronunciation Model

In order to properly train HMMs, and thus accurately recognize any arbitrary sequence of words in an utterance, each word must be represented as a sequence of the basic speech sounds, phonemes, and eventually by the sequence of the corresponding HMMs. The word *tomato*, for example, would be represented by the following sequence of contextual HMMs.

?_**t**_o t_**o**_m m_**ey**_t ey_**t**_o t_**o**_?

The question marks here represent any potential phonemes at the end of any possible previous and following word in the utterance, including a possible pause. Moreover, as we know, some words may have different pronunciations. Tomato, as is often noted, even in a classic American song, can also be pronounced as

?_**t**_o t_**o**_m m_**ah**_t ah_**t**_o t_**o**_?

It is clear, therefore, that in order to be recognized, any word in the vocabulary must be represented by a number of possible pronunciations and potential juncture and pauses between the previous and following word.[22] This is known as a *pronunciation model*, and in classic speech recognition systems it is generally built as the example describes, based on phonetic knowledge of the language in question.

Language Model

Not all sequences of words are possible in a language. In fact, if you consider all the random combinations of words in a defined vocabulary in all possible sequences of arbitrary length, you get an infinite number of them, of which only a tiny fraction are legitimate sentences of a language—what linguists would call *grammatical* sentences. A language model is a way to define what the possible, or likely, sequences of words are.

A grammar—and we will see grammars in more detail in chapter 4, on natural language understanding—is a practical way to describe all of the possible, and only, grammatical sentences in a defined domain. However, a grammar is primarily used when the number of possible sentences is limited, and we are quite sure users would speak *in grammar*; in other words, they would not speak utterances that are outside those described by the grammar itself. If what the user speaks is out of grammar, the speech recognizer will not be able to recognize it, or will mistakenly recognize it as some in-grammar sentence that is close enough, but different from what the user actually spoke. For a speech recognizer that should be able to recognize pretty much any arbitrary utterance, as for dictation or Speech2Text, grammars thus are not always an effective solution.

Since the early days of statistically based speech recognition, the idea was to use a statistical language model (rather than a grammar) that would assign a probability to any sequence of words reflecting the probability of finding that sequence in the actual usage of the language. Thus less frequent or nearly impossible sequences of words would be downplayed by the recognition process in favor of sequences that are more likely to be uttered. In other words, for a properly trained statistical language model, the sentence "Lions are dangerous animals" would have a higher chance of being recognized than the sentence "Animals dangerous lions are" because the second sentence is totally uncommon in English. Similarly, the phrase "recognize speech" would have a higher probability than the very uncommon phrase "wreck a nice beach," even though both of them are grammatical. While these two utterances may be confusable acoustically, when using a properly trained language model, a speech recognizer would have a bias toward the former phrase, rather than the latter, because it has a higher probability.

Now the problem to solve is building a model that allows us to calculate the probability of any possible sequence of words, such as "lions are dangerous animals" as well as "animals dangerous lions are," even though the latter phrase is never observed in practice. (except for twice in this book). The solution comes from the probability theory that—under proper assumptions—estimates the probability of an arbitrary and long string of words based on the probabilities of shorter segments.[23] These shorter segments traditionally consist of three words and are called *trigrams*.[24] So, we can calculate the probability of "lions are dangerous animals" based on the probabilities of:

<start of sentence> lions are

lions are dangerous

are dangerous animals

dangerous animals <end of sentence>

Given large amounts of text, those probabilities are easier to estimate than those of longer sequences of words. Because of the vast amount of text available on the web, accessing large, nearly unlimited amounts of text is not a problem. However, even with millions and millions of passages, a large number of trigrams, or higher-order n-grams, may not ever be found. Thus the estimation of n-grams needs to provide a way to determine the probability of those sequences that have never been observed, but may appear in practice. By using a powerful language model, a recognizer can be biased toward most likely utterances, and reduce the likelihood of trivial errors.

Search

Search is at the core of the statistical speech recognition algorithm. The goal of the search module is to find the sequence of words that, based on the acoustic, phonetic, and language models, is most likely to correspond to the sequence of feature vectors of the input utterance. Let's see what that means.

Start by taking a random sequence of words from the vocabulary and calculate its probability using the language model. Then substitute each word with the corresponding sequence of phonemes. Many words may have more than one representation (remember /tomahto/ and /tomayto/), and you should also consider the phonetic variations at the juncture (remember /you all/ and /y'all/). Computer scientists can represent all these variations in a compact form, possibly as a graph, and also take into account the probabilities of different phonetic variations that may have been calculated beforehand on a large corpus of utterances. Put everything together and now you have a graph where every path, from the beginning to the end, corresponds to a particular realization of sequences of phonemes representing the chosen, random sequence of words. At this point you can represent each phoneme in the graph with the corresponding HMM. The result is an even larger graph of statistical models, which is still a substantial composite HMM. You now take the sequence of feature vectors corresponding to input utterance, and compute its probability using the composite HMM. If you have followed the logic so far, you may realize that that probability corresponds to the probability that your sequence of feature vectors—your input utterance—is an utterance of the random sequence of words you chose at the beginning of the process.

Now imagine you do all of the preceding for all possible arbitrary sequences of words of any arbitrary length. When you are finished, if you choose the sequence of words with the highest probability, you can assume that it is the most likely sequence of words that was spoken.

Obviously, this process is quite inefficient, especially considering that with a finite vocabulary there are infinite arbitrary sequences of words of arbitrary length. However, computer scientists have found very efficient ways to search for the best path in a graph of virtually unlimited size.[25]

For half a century, speech recognition technology has been following the statistical approach with an accuracy that allowed commercial deployment of a number of services, such as customer care or dictation. Scientists have been working for decades to continue to improve accuracy through better models, better feature-based representation, and more efficient search. In fact each component of the classical ASR architecture of figure 2 has been associated with a specific branch of research and technological specialization for decades.

Training a Speech Recognizer
As for all machine learning systems, a critical factor that determines the accuracy of statistical speech recognition is training set size and variety. If we want to build a Speech2Text system able to recognize an almost unlimited variety of words and expressions in a given language, we need to make sure that the training set includes enough utterances to represent all possible variability of all speech sounds. As we know, the main causes of speech variability

are the physiological differences among the speakers, including their gender and age, as well as their speaking habits, including their accent and pronunciation idiosyncrasies. In the design and collection of a training set for speech recognition it is also important to consider the variety of acoustic and noise situations that may affect the incoming speech. That includes the different types of collection devices—phones and smartphones, for instance—that will be used in the application. With the advent of home devices, such as Amazon Echo and Google Home, which collect speech from a distance (typically referred to as far-field speech), it is important to include utterances collected from near and far ranges, and consider different types of acoustic environments, such as a quiet or a noisy room, and different levels of reverberation. Even the type of noise arising when using an assistant in a car must be considered.

Once a large amount of speech is available for training, in order to apply supervised machine learning each utterance needs to be labeled with the words that have been spoken in a process called *transcription*. Modern speech recognizers, based on HMM acoustic modeling (or neural networks, to be discussed later), do not require the transcriptions to mark the exact point in each utterance where each word begins and ends. They do not even require, to a certain extent, the annotation of whether there is a pause or not between two consecutive words, or the correct phonetics of words (e.g., /tomahto/ vs. / tomeyto/) or co-articulation (e.g., you all vs. /y'all/). The only annotation needed is the correct sequence of words spoken in each utterance. This generally is accomplished with the help of human transcribers who listen to each utterance and write what they hear. Of course, transcribing millions of utterances would be a daunting job, but the cost of that can be alleviated by using a combination of crowdsourcing and semi-automated procedures. For early speech recognizers, the collection of training utterances was done explicitly by hiring subjects who were instructed to speak a number of prescribed utterances into a microphone, in an acoustically controlled room. So, the transcribers knew in advance what each recorded utterance was supposed to be, and their job was to correct the transcription in case the subject spoke different words by mistake.

In recent years, with automatic speech recognition now widely deployed, some of the speech collected by the systems in operation has been used as a training set to continue to improve ASR performance. Today, however, with the increased global awareness of the need to protect user privacy, and responsible companies committing to do so, ASR technology is rapidly moving toward reducing and eventually eliminating the need for transcribed speech, for instance by using synthetic speech.[26]

Language models also need to be trained based on data. Generally, because modern ASRs must recognize words from a vocabulary of hundreds of thousands, and often a million or more words, the amount of data required for language models is orders of magnitude larger than that required for acoustic models.[27] Since language models are not influenced by the variability of the speech signal, their training can be accomplished using large corpora of text. For general speech recognition one can consider, for instance, all text found on the web, from newspapers, magazines, Wikipedia, public blogs and discussion groups, and more. The vast amount of text available on the web provides practically unlimited amounts of data for training language models for many world languages.

End-to-End Speech Recognition

While research scientists have been investigating the use of DNNs to approach each of the components of the classic speech recognizer of figure 4, a more attractive idea was to combine all of them in a single end-to-end neural network. The vision is to create a large DNN that could learn the whole process of speech recognition, from speech to words, without having to break it into a number of distinct components that need to be optimized independently. In fact, there are several successful attempts to develop end-to-end recognizers that take the speech waveform as input and produce words expressed as characters, some of them already used in practical applications.[28] The regularity and homogeneity of end-to-end systems allow scientists to make them smaller in terms of number of parameters and computer memory, without drastically affecting their accuracy; this process is called *distillation*. In 2019 Google shipped the new Pixel 4 smartphone that includes a *distilled* end-to-end speech recognizer capable of recognizing hundreds of thousands of words.

It is now clear that end-to-end speech recognition is today's mainstream evolution of speech recognition, a technology that has fascinated researchers and technologists for decades, from the first analogic machines in the 1950s to today's deep learning systems. Yet there are still a lot of problems to solve, such as recognizing speech accurately in highly noisy and reverberant situations or when it comes from speakers with strong accents, using contextual knowledge about the speaker and the environment to improve speech understanding accuracy, learning new words never encountered before, and so on. Research is continuing to innovate to make sure the capabilities of automatic speech recognition technology will evolve to get closer and closer to those of humans.

NATURAL LANGUAGE
UNDERSTANDING

Why do we need natural language understanding (NLU)? To appreciate the need and the complexity of an NLU module for a virtual assistant, let's start with a simple example. Imagine you want to build a system with one purpose: to dial telephone numbers by voice. And imagine you have an ASR system that can transcribe everything you say into words. The system prompts you to speak a telephone number, and just a telephone number. If you do so, the ASR will transcribe your utterance exactly as a string of digits, most likely the one corresponding to the telephone number you just spoke. You pass that to a dialing module, and all is done. No natural language understanding is needed to interpret a string of digits.

Let's up the ante and build a slightly more sophisticated system that allows you to frame your string of digits into a sentence. Now you may need some string processing to extract the telephone number and disregard the *fluff*, that is, the words that do not carry any meaning for a phone dialing application. Of course, assuming that the only thing you are expected to do is to dial a number, anything else you say besides a telephone number is irrelevant and can be disregarded. For example, if you speak:

Please dial 5 5 5 7 3 2 1 2 1 2 thanks.

One can write a very simple string editing program to remove from the string returned by the ASR everything that is not a digit, and send the result to the dialing module that will fulfill the requested action. Of course, the sequence of digits may not be a real telephone number. Instead of seven or ten digits, the typical length of a telephone number in the United States, you may speak a different number of digits, or no digits at all. But for the time being, let's disregard this possibility.

Now let's build a more complicated virtual assistant that can execute additional operations besides dialing, such as storing a number, retrieving the contact information, or sending a message to a number. Here are related utterances that you would like your virtual assistant to understand.

Dial 5 5 5 7 3 2 1 2 1 2.

Send a message to 5 5 5 7 3 2 1 2 1 2.

Retrieve contact information for 5 5 5 7 3 2 1 2 1 2.

Save 5 5 5 7 3 2 1 2 1 2.

This is also a very simple system, and you can get away with some string manipulation. You can detect the sequence of digits in the text returned by the ASR, and find a match of the remaining words in a table of possible commands. But of course, unless users are instructed to speak exactly the required words, you need to consider all of the possible variations that they can naturally speak. For instance

Please phone 5 5 5 7 3 2 1 2 1 2.

Would you call the number 5 5 5 7 3 2 1 2 1 2?

Send text to 5 5 5 7 3 2 1 2 1 2.

Get me the information for 5 5 5 7 3 2 1 2 1 2?

Who is 5 5 5 7 3 2 1 2 1 2?

Store 5 5 5 7 3 2 1 2 1 2 as my mom's telephone number.

5 5 5 7 3 2 1 2 1 2 is a telephone number that I would like you to store for me.

You can probably still get away with some more sophisticated string manipulation that takes into account all possible variations of the allowed commands, but now you understand that even for a small number of commands, you need to start requiring a solution that can scale to a potential unlimited and unpredictable number of sentence variations. That's what an NLU system is for. The examples we've discussed so far refer to fairly basic systems that can execute perhaps half a dozen different commands. Imagine the complexity that arises when the number of commands grows to dozens, hundreds, or more.

The complexity of the language needed to control a virtual assistant grows with its functionality. Imagine now that you want to build a virtual assistant or a robot that can execute a large number of different commands that can no longer be encoded as a direct mapping between keywords and actions. Imagine modern virtual assistants—such as Siri, Alexa, and Google Assistant—performing a range of actions from responding to queries about the weather forecast at a particular time in a particular country or city, to controlling your home automation devices, playing specific music, ordering flowers for your mom's birthday, or responding to all sorts of general-knowledge questions. The number of potential queries can become so large that it's practically unlimited. Adding up all the possible ways you can express yourself, it is easy to realize how there are potentially infinite utterances from which an assistant should be able to extract the meaning with the goal of executing the requested action. If you want the assistant to be able to understand anything a user may say, you need to implement something more sophisticated than a mapping between all the possible sentences and all the possible meanings, especially considering this would require a mapping table of infinite size. NLU systems try to address this problem in many different ways.

Language is a mechanism that conveys meaning through loosely structured sequences of words. The grammatical rules of a language somewhat prescribe how to express meaning with words. But grammatical rules often present a number of exceptions and irregularities. People use idiomatic forms that escape a rigid formalism, and metaphors that should not be interpreted literally. Often we are able to understand highly nongrammatical expressions from people with a limited knowledge of the language, such as young children or foreigners. Words have synonyms, and there are many words that are intrinsically ambiguous. Moreover, when we talk to machines, we often use a simple schematic language that we learned by doing web searches. Sentence fragments such as "restaurants around here" are acceptable rather than the more formal and lengthier "Would you please give me a list of the restaurants situated around the place where I am now?" In addition to the language expressions' intrinsic variability, we need to consider the combinatorics deriving from the arbitrary order of the phrases expressing different concepts in a single complex utterance. For instance, if we are searching for a flight with Delta Airlines from New York to San Francisco early in the morning on June 27, we can freely specify the flight requirements in any order, including:

A flight to San Francisco on the 27th of June with Delta airlines leaving New York early in the morning.

An early morning flight from New York to San Francisco with Delta on June 27th.

A flight with Delta from New York early in the morning of June 27th, going to San Francisco.

Furthermore, one can express some of the elements of a request using other requests, and combine them in a single utterance. For example, if I would have to get to San Francisco a few hours earlier than my dinner appointment with my friend Jon, assuming that the hypothetical assistant knows the appointments on my calendar, I could say:

A flight with Delta from New York arriving in San
Francisco at least 2 hours before my dinner with Jon.

That's called *conceptual composition* and makes understanding natural language even more complex.

In contrast to the unlimited combinatorial and compositional variety of natural language, one could represent
meanings by using a symbolic formulation that a computer
program can unambiguously and univocally interpret to
execute the request. We can define NLU as the process of
translating any meaningful string of words into a well-
defined formal computer language designed to represent
its meanings—or its *semantics*—specifically defined for
the application in question.

In order to better understand the difference between
natural language text and its meaning representation,
let's go through a simple example and make the following
request to a hypothetical virtual assistant:

Make a reservation at an Italian restaurant around
here for four people tomorrow in the early evening.

This is a relatively complex request and it cannot be
readily used to feed an automated system for an online
restaurant reservation. Online restaurant reservation systems require a quite structured representation, such as:

NLU is the process of translating any meaningful string of words into a well-defined formal computer language designed to represent its meanings—or its *semantics*—specifically defined for the application in question.

Date: 7-14-2019

Time: 7:00 PM

Number-of-people: 4

Location: West Village, New York, NY

Type-of-cuisine: Italian

The job of an NLU system is to translate the original natural language sentence into the preceding symbolic representation—in other words, to estimate the values of variables, such as `Date`, `Time`, and `Number-of-people`.

However, that translation is not without its problems. First, the restaurant reservation system requires a date, but a date is not clearly expressed by the user who indicates the day of the event simply as a colloquial "tomorrow" and the time is also expressed vaguely as "early evening." Finally the location is totally missing in the request. A proper NLU needs to be able to resolve these issues while managing the intrinsic variability and ambiguity of language. In fact, you can certainly come up with many different utterances expressing the same concepts in different forms.

Before going into more detail regarding the meaning representation, let's summarize what we have learned so far:

• An automatic speech recognizer (ASR) transcribes an utterance into a textual representation of the sequence of words spoken.

• A natural language understanding (NLU) system translates a textual sequence of words into a symbolic univocal representation of its meaning.

So, now we have two sources of potential errors for a virtual assistant. The ASR can misrecognize or miss some of the words, or even introduce spurious ones. Even if the ASR does a good job, the NLU may not be able to understand the meaning correctly. These two sources of errors affect the overall performance of any virtual assistant.

Meaning Representation

The first problem we encounter in building an NLU system is the definition of a proper and univocal representation of the meaning that can be used by a computer to execute a command, respond to a question, or perform a task.

Let's go back to our restaurant reservation example. Generally the purpose of an utterance is the expression of an intent. The intent in our example is clearly to make a restaurant reservation. Such clarity is not always the case, and often an intent needs to be induced by the knowledge of the context. For instance, if I jump into a taxi in New York City, and I say "JFK," the driver clearly understands that my intent is "drive me to the JFK airport." Think of speaking the same expression when you are in a store, such as a pharmacy. People will look at you, puzzled, trying to guess what you mean.

In computer terms an intent can be expressed as a variable and its associated value, such as

```
intent = make-restaurant-reservation.
```

Additionally, as we saw earlier, a restaurant reservation needs values for a number of variables, often called *arguments* or *entities*, to be completely specified, such as date, time, number of people, location, and cuisine. And of course, different intents have different sets of arguments.

If you want to build a system that understands anything a user could say, you have to start by creating an inventory of all possible intents. The list of possible intents that a human language can express is obviously very large, arguably unlimited. However, for practical applications, we need to limit the list of intents to those that the virtual assistant is designed to fulfill. In today's systems, that list of intents still needs to be handcrafted and maintained by the system developers. That's one of the main problems with natural language understanding. If you want an assistant to understand thousands of intents, all of them and their specific arguments need to be crafted by human experts, and maintained in an intent schema, which is often called an *ontology*. Unfortunately there is no universal ontology that all the developers of NLU systems can use and share. Every system would have to have its own, and depending on its scale, it may require the labor of many specialized developers, with the potential introduction of duplications and inconsistencies.

Let's keep in mind that human language can express more than one intent in a single utterance, but for the sake of this discussion we will assume that a user speaks only one intent at a time.

Once we have crafted an intent schema, the next step is developing algorithms that map the words in an utterance to the exact intent they express and its arguments. The most traditional way to do that is based on formal grammars expressed by what is known as a context-free formalism.[1] A context-free grammar is a series of rules that define well-formed, grammatical sentences, based on combinations of words and references to other rules. In computer science, the words in a grammar rule are called *terminals*, and the references to other rules are called *nonterminals*.

Let's look at a very simple example of a context-free grammar. For instance, if you want to define the intent *make-restaurant-reservation*, you can start with the following rule (notice that the rules and the nonterminals are indicated by a dollar sign preceding the symbol):

```
$make-restaurant-reservation =
    make a reservation at $restaurant-
    type for $number-of-people $date at
    $time
```

Then we can add rules that define the arguments, for example for the type of restaurant:

```
$restaurant-type = ((an Italian)
| (a Chinese) | (a Mexican) |
(an American)) restaurant
```

Notice that we used the symbol |, called *disjunction*, to represent alternatives (you can read it as the conjunction *or*). For every type of restaurant we use the correct indefinite article (*a* or *an*) as required by the next word. Furthermore, we use parentheses to group things. Similarly:

```
$number-of-people = ((1 [person]) |

((2 | 3 | 4 | 5 | 6) [people]))

$date = today | tomorrow |
$structured-date
```

```
$time = ((early | late) (afternoon |
evening)) |
$structured-time
```

The square brackets [ ] are used to indicate optional elements (e.g., *person* or *people*). You can also notice that the rules make reference to other nonterminals, which we would have to define to describe the language expressions for structured dates and times, such as *March twenty-seventh*, or *seven-thirty pm*.[2]

Context-free notations used in practical NLU systems allow for even more sophisticated ways to express grammars in a compact form.[3] They also enable embedding programming code in the rules to transform the words that make up a segment into some other form that can more readily be used to fulfill the requested action. For instance, one can embed code into the $date rule to calculate the date corresponding to today or tomorrow based on the current date, or convert expressions such as early evening into a predefined time interval. Doing these conversions inside the grammar is possible using snippets of embedded programs (typically JavaScript), as allowed by the grammar formalism, even though it may not be the best architectural choice.[4]

While formal grammars can be a powerful way to represent a number of possible sentences and phrases related to an intent, they may not be the most efficient. In fact, there are two problems with grammars. The first is that every possible variation needs to be accurately accounted for. As we saw, in complex requests a user can speak the intent arguments in pretty much any order, and the grammar needs to account for that along with the possible word variations. Thus the set of rules can become very large and complicated. Writing and maintaining grammars that cover all the possible combinations and variations of what users can say is generally a cumbersome job, typically done by linguists or trained grammar developers who have a good mastery of the particular language for which the assistant is built.

The second problem with formal grammars is related to the fact that when we speak we often include words that are not contributing directly to the overall meaning. We refer to those expressions as *fluff* or *filler words*. For instance, rather than the simple "make a reservation," one could say "I would like to make a reservation" or "please make a reservation" or "would you please make a reservation, thanks," and so on, in an almost endless number of possibilities. In general, pleasantries and other expressions that would make an utterance sound natural may be removed without impacting its content.[5] Additionally, when we speak in a conversational manner we often introduce disfluencies and nongrammatical constructs that do not generally appear in well-formed text. Moreover the

ASR transcription may include spurious words or mistakes that do not necessarily disrupt the original meaning. *Robust parsing* is a solution to that set of problems.

The idea of robust parsing was first developed in the early 1990s when the US speech recognition community faced, for the first time, a formal evaluation of speech understanding systems built according to well-defined requirements. The US DARPA (the Defense Advanced Research Projects Agency that had been called ARPA until 1972) established a program called ATIS (Air Travel Information System). Different research centers participating in the program competed by building and regularly evaluating their versions of a virtual assistant to answer flight-related questions.[6] The first attempts to use formal grammars to parse the output of speech did not produce satisfactory results. In fact the grammars were developed by linguists to parse written text, but speech includes disfluencies, hems and haws, long pauses, false starts, repetitions, and other hard-to-predict phenomena that cannot be easily modeled by a formal grammar.

To address this, many labs came up with the idea of a robust parser. Rather than attempting to define all the words in a sentence, a robust parser leaves *holes,* or *wildcards*, for words that do not contribute to the meaning. Robust parsers can also allow for different concepts representing the arguments of a request, to appear in any order.

One could capture the grammar previously discussed in a robust parsing fashion, with the following notation:

```
$make-restaurant-reservation =
    $any-words reservation ($any-words
    $concept)+
```

The rule `$any-words` would match any possible arbitrary sequence of words and `$concept` can be any of `$date`, `$time`, `$number-of-people`, `$type-of-restaurant`. The symbol + after the parenthesis denotes the repetition of the previous expression one or more times; in other words, it's a compact notation for the following unlimited set of rules:

```
$make-restaurant-reservation = $any-
words $concept
```

```
$make-restaurant-reservation = $any-
words $concept $any-words $concept
```

```
$make-restaurant-reservation =
    $any-words $concept $any-words
    $concept $any-words $concept . . .
```

The risk with a robust parser is that it may mistakenly accept nonsensical utterances. It easy to see that the preceding rules will also parse sentences such as:

Like I make a reservation at seven thirty at nine pm today at an Italian restaurant tomorrow tomorrow.

This, of course, does not make any sense. If the parser developer is not careful, it could also accept a meaningful sentence, such as

I want to make a reservation for tonight, but not at an Italian restaurant,

. . . but then mistakenly parse it to mean that the user actually wanted an Italian restaurant.

However, there are a few considerations that we should keep in mind:

- Nonsensical sentences are rarely spoken.

- Negations, as in the preceding Italian restaurant example, can be accounted for in the design of the parser.

- Systems based on robust parsing generally have heuristics that prevent the parser from accepting nonsensical utterances.

Of course a robust parser can introduce more mistakes than a strict formal grammar The more flexibility we have in the parser the more sentences it will accept that deviate from the intended meaning. In technical terms we say that the parser *overgenerates*, meaning that the language it represents includes a large number of sentences that may not have the desired meaning. However, depending on the application, and based on a careful crafting, robust parsers have proven more useful than their limitations would suggest.

In any case, writing grammars or robust parsers requires a lot of human labor by dedicated people, typically language specialists, who constantly monitor the accuracy metrics of the NLU and add rules whenever needed. It is indeed the reality that, while research is looking at better ways to perform NLU, including via machine learning, a number of today's virtual assistants may still include some handcrafted grammars.

Statistical Natural Language Understanding

In the early 1990s some researchers started to experiment with statistical learning systems for NLU. My colleagues and I developed the first of those systems at Bell Laboratories.[7] The data-driven system, called CHRONUS (Conceptual Hidden Representation of Natural Unconstrained Speech), eventually outperformed all the grammar-based methods in the DARPA ATIS program.[8] CHRONUS extended the idea of HMMs to represent not only sequences of words, but also sequences of conceptual entities—something very similar to intents and their arguments—each associated with statistical language models. The system could learn from training data that needed to be annotated with the correct intent and arguments. In a way, the conceptual HMM system was a statistical form of robust parsing. Another interesting system developed in the 1990s cast NLU as the problem of translating between natural language and the formal language representing the meaning, then successfully used statistical machine translation to solve it.[9] Many different techniques were experimented, but the idea that NLU was a problem that could be solved using ML started to become mainstream.

Many research efforts revolved around ATIS, which was for many years the only available and most extensive corpus for experimenting with new NLU technologies while providing objective evaluation metrics. At the same time the industry was rapidly evolving toward the development of telephone-based speech recognition applications for customer care. As we saw in chapter 3, the advent of VoiceXML fostered the birth of the speech IVR industry and the proliferation of complex telephone-based virtual assistants with specific customer-care goals.

It is important to note that for telephone IVRs the NLU component was deeply integrated within the ASR. In other words, while research focused on developing sophisticated ML systems for NLU, the industry was still using context-free grammars, like the one described earlier, to constrain the speech recognizer to the phrases requested by the prompts. If the user said something different, the speech recognizer would either reject that or erroneously output one of the sentences prescribed by the grammar.

However, as we saw earlier, it was a good industrial practice to accurately craft the prompt to lead users to answers that are covered by the grammars. Thus the chance of a user saying something that the grammar could not account for is small for directed dialog systems, but not insignificant. For instance, if at a certain point in the dialog the system required a user to choose among a number of alternatives, a well-designed prompt would sound like:

Please choose one of the following: account information, transfer funds, mortgage rates, or say other.

At this point most of the callers would say one of the prompted keywords. However, there is always a chance that someone will ignore the prompt and say

I am calling because I see this strange charge added to my account and I don't know what it is.

In the best possible scenario, a grammar-constrained ASR would be able to reject any recognition hypothesis that does not belong to the underlying grammar.[10] In technical terms this is called a *no-match* result.

However, not all customer care problems could be solved by giving users a number of options to choose from. Sometimes the number of choices would be too large to instruct a user on what to say. A situation like that is exemplified by the problem of *call routing*.

Imagine the initial prompt of an IVR like this: "Please tell me the reason you are calling about, so as I can route you to the right agent." That is technically called an *open prompt*, a prompt that does not suggest what to say but opens up the possibility for a user to describe the reason for the call in her own words. A non-open-prompt strategy, called *directed prompt*, will not work here. The number of alternatives to suggest may be so large that multiple hierarchical menus are required, which could be cumbersome for callers. And even if multiple menus are possible, some of the choices may not make sense for the users, who may have trouble knowing what to choose, or choose randomly. In those situations the best approach is to let users describe the problem in their own words and then match what they say to one of the choices. This is a classification problem that can be solved by machine learning.

The idea of using data-driven techniques for call routing, or similar open-prompt problems, originated at AT&T Labs in the late 1990s where an experimental technology called "How May I Help You?" (HMIHY) was developed.[11] The researchers who developed HMIHY collected a large number of utterances from users calling a customer care number and responding to the "How may I help you?" recorded prompt. While users thought they were talking to a computer, the calls actually were monitored by human operators who promptly switched the caller to the correct department based on their understanding of the problem.[12] In this way the A&T researchers amassed a large collection of utterances, each tagged with the presumably correct department, or destination, handling the caller's request.[13] This is a perfect problem for supervised machine-learning classifiers that can learn from the tagged corpus how to associate the correct destination, or route, to any arbitrary request. Of course the accuracy of the classifier depends on the amount of training data, the limitations of the ML classifier in use, and eventually the design of the categories and how distinguishable they are solely on the basis of the user description.

After the results of the "How May I Help You?" experiment became public, the industry of voice IVR systems started to deploy similar approaches for call routing and other open-prompt problems. For example, at SpeechCycle we used statistical machine learning to classify the user responses to the open prompt question "What problem are you calling about?" into a number of symptom categories, each mapped to one of a predefined list of problems and their resolutions.[14]

The evolution of virtual agents proved that ML classifiers can be used effectively to map the ASR transcription of a user's utterance to a category that represents the intent. However, complex utterances are not made of intents only, but, as we saw, often include a number of arguments. In fact intent classification and argument extraction are two problems of a different nature. While the former entails assigning an utterance to one of many categories, the latter requires the detection of a phrase within the utterance, the extraction of the relevant information, and the mapping of this information to a canonical form. Most of the arguments are what computational linguists call *named entities*. A named entity is an object such as a date, a proper name, a city, a time, an amount of money, and so forth. Fortunately, named entities have a structured syntax or alternatively belong to a known list of textual elements, such as the names of cities or days of the week. The extraction of named entities is a problem that has been solved with different degrees of success by statistical classifiers, and more recently by deep neural networks (DNNs).[15]

Deep Learning for Natural Language Understanding

The success of DNNs in different areas such as ASR and machine translation motivated the exploration of deep learning methods for NLU. NLU is a problem of sequential nature: a DNN solution needs to map a sequence of words of arbitrary length corresponding to the input utterance, to a corresponding set of symbols of arbitrary size, meaning one or more intents and a number of arguments. As we discussed earlier regarding end-to-end speech recognition, the solution of this problem can rely on some form of recurrent neural network.

A simple example could help to demonstrate what a recurrent DNN solution to the NLU problem would look like. At the input layer of a neural network we have a sequence of words, possibly coming from the speech recognizer. The goal for the other end, the output layer, is to get one or more symbols denoting intents and possible arguments. Let's start from the output layer. For the sake of simplicity, let's focus on the classification of any arbitrary sequence of words into one of the following six intents:

1. `switch-lights-on`

2. `switch-lights-off`

3. `increase-ambient-temperature`

4. `decrease-ambient-temperature`

5. `lock-door`

6. `unlock-door`

So, the output of the neural network may be configured to have exactly six neurons, one for each of these six intents. The neuron that produces the highest value, after the network processes the input sentence, will be the network's best guess of the intent represented by the input words.

Let's see now how the input layer of the network would handle the input words. The simplest way is to allocate one input neuron for each possible word at a specific position in the sentence. Unfortunately, the set of all words of a language is unlimited. You can consider a thousand, ten thousand, a million words and there is always a new word that we have not considered. New words are created every day. Think of the word *Brexit*—it didn't even exist a few years ago. There is also an infinitely growing variety of people's first and last names, company and product names, acronyms, and so on. Therefore, if we want to build a practical NLU system, we need to choose a reasonable set of words in widespread use. For the sake of this example, let's consider a small vocabulary of 1,000 words, and assume that any user sentences would include words only from that set. If we order those 1,000 words in some arbitrary way, for instance, alphabetically, we can establish a correspondence between each word and each of 1,000 input neurons. So the first neuron, neuron number 1, would represent the first word in the vocabulary, let's say the word *about*, and the last neuron, neuron number 1,000, would represent the last word in our vocabulary, let's say the word *zone*. In this manner we represent the set of 1,000 input neurons as a list of numbers—called a vector in computer jargon. Thus every word in our input sentence is represented as a vector of all 0s except for a 1 for the position that corresponds to that word. And the values, 0s or 1s, also correspond to the values given to the 1,000 input neurons. This coding convention is called *one-hot*.

Now, let's go back to our example and imagine that the input sentence is "Please switch the lights on." If we look at our 1,000-word vocabulary, *please* happens to be word number 634 in our ordering, *switch* is word 714, *the* is word 966, *lights* is word 489, and *on* is word 558. So, when the first word is presented to the network, all the input neurons will be given a value of 0, except for neuron number 634, corresponding to the word *please*, which will be given a value of 1. For the second word, all the input neurons will be set to 0, except for neuron number 714. And so on. After we have processed the last word, we would like to see the output neuron number 1, corresponding to the intent `switch-lights-on`, have the highest value among all the other output neurons. That would indicate that the network has understood that the meaning of the utterance corresponds to intent number 1.

But as we know, that would not work, because each time we present a new word to the input layer and activate the neuron corresponding to that word, if we don't do anything different than what is done in regular neural networks, the parameter learning process will start from scratch and forget the processing done for the previous word. At the end, therefore, when all the words have been consumed by the input layer, the output would be influenced only by the last word in the sentence. As we saw in chapter 3, one way to make our neural network output depend on all the input words consists in influencing the processing of each word with the network results of the previous words. That means making the neural network recurrent. One way to do that, but not the only and most sophisticated way, consists in sending the output of the hidden neurons obtained while processing one word, also called a *thought vector*, back to the network while it is processing the next word.

What I described here is a very simple recurrent network, rarely used today in practical applications. Rather, especially for NLU, we use more complex networks that try to relax some of the limitations of the simple architecture. For instance, we discussed LSTMs (long short-term memory) networks earlier. One of the problems with language is that there are *long-distance* phenomena that affect large spans of a sentence. An example of that is the phenomenon of gender and number agreement that is present in many different languages. For example, consider the sentence: "When I saw Mary walking in front of the bear I screamed and told her to turn back." The pronoun *her* toward the end is clearly related to *Mary* in the first part of the sentence. Since *Mary* is a feminine proper noun, any pronominal reference, at least for the English language, needs to match the feminine gender. If the person I saw was *John*, the correct pronoun would have been *him*. And if I wanted to refer to the bear, I would have used the pronoun *it*. Now, there are ten words in the sentence between *Mary* and *her*. In any simple recurrent network the effect of the word *Mary* would be forgotten by the time the network starts processing the word *her*. And by *forgotten* I mean that the computational effect of the word *Mary* would probably be negligible by the time the recurrent network is processing the word *her*.

Gender and number agreement are not the only long distance phenomena of languages. For instance, in the following question "When does the flight that leaves London at 8:30 am arrive in Milan?" the first part of the sentence, *When does*, suggests that the request is about a time, but only the last part of the sentence, *arrives in Milan* identifies that the question is about the arrival time and not, for instance, the departure time. Again, there are eight words between the initial question and its qualifier *arrives*, and any simple recurrent network would not be able to connect the two and decide that the intent is related to the arrival time and not the departure time. Other languages, such as German and Dutch, have more important long-distance relationships between the words in a sentence, such as the determination of the meaning of a verb based on the verb particle at the end of the sentence.

Recently, a sophisticated new technique developed by Google research scientists and called BERT (Bidirectional Encoder Representations for Transformers) produces state-of-the-art results on standard test sets.[16] BERT is attracting the attention of many researchers in the natural language field.

However, commercial assistants still use a combination of structured methods such as grammars and robust parsers and DNNs. As this book is written, no mainstream method exists yet to implement NLU for complex commercial assistants. How to build the optimal NLU that scales to a large number of intents with minimal human labor is an open question that researchers continue to try to answer.

Word Embeddings

In this section we will discuss a technique to encode words in a more effective way than one-hot. That technique, generally called *word embedding*, has been developed and become mainstream over the past decade and was inspired by the concept of distributional semantics and early work in that area by Joshua Bengio.[17]

As we saw earlier, one-hot is a simple way to encode words as numeric inputs by assigning a specific position in a list, or vector, to each word of the vocabulary. That position is based on an arbitrary ordering (such as alpha-betical) that does not have any association with the actual usage and meaning of the word. Once the position of each word in the list is established, each position is associated with an input neuron that is activated when the word is present in a sentence.

The one-hot coding has two problems. The first is that it is not very efficient. If you have a vocabulary of ten thousand words, you would need ten thousand input neurons, only one of them being activated at a time. And if you have a million words, which is not uncommon, you need a million input neurons. If you want to add one or more words to the vocabulary, then you need to add one or more input neurons to the input layer, and retrain the network. This is not very practical.

The second problem is that the one-hot representation does not address how words are used in a language and their semantic similarity. Let's say you have two words that can be used interchangeably in a sentence. For instance, in the preceding examples, you can use the word *turn* instead of *switch* without changing the meaning of the sentence: "Switch the lights on" in this context has the same meaning as "Turn the lights on." For the network to learn that the two sentences have the same meaning, you need to train it with examples of both. Considering all the possible semantically similar words, and having cor-responding examples for a large number of meanings, and a large number of words, may not be feasible. Thus the resulting network will not be able to generalize to semantically similar words that have not been seen in similar examples in training corpus.

Going back to our example, it is clear that the words *turn* and *switch* have a high semantic similarity, at least in that particular domain. That's equivalent to saying that they exhibit a small *semantic distance*. How about words like *cat* and *lion*? They are not as semantically similar, and totally interchangeable, as *turn* and *switch* are. In general, one will not find them as an alternative in any sentence, as in "Lions live in the savanna." However, they can be interchangeable in some contexts, as in "Lions are felines." So, their semantic distance is not as small as the distance between turn and switch, but not as large as between train and cat. This leads to the realization that all words are related, and there might exist a multidimensional space where, if we represent words as points, the distance between *turn* and *switch* is smaller than the distance between *cat* and *lion* which is smaller than the distance between *cat* and *train*.

Let's go back for a minute to the one-hot representation. If we consider the vectors of 0s and 1s representing each word in our 1,000 word example, the geometric distance between any two words in a space with 1,000 dimensions is always 1, no matter how semantically similar the two words are.

Word embeddings and related techniques such as words-to-vectors are ways to represent each word with a vector of numbers of fixed size, regardless of how many words are in the vocabulary. The elements of those vectors are not just 1s and 0s, but could be any number. The distance of two arbitrary vectors, in other words the distance between the corresponding points in a multidimensional space where each dimension corresponds to an element of the vectors, is related to the semantic distance between the corresponding words.

How can we determine if two words are semantically similar? One way to do that is to measure how interchangeable they are in a sentence, or in other words how frequently they appear in the same context of words to the left, and to the right. Thus for the words *turn* and *switch* we may find a number of contexts where the use of both words is similar—that is, they are interchangeable, such as "turn the lights on," "switch the lights on"—and where the words have different usage; for instance, you can say "turn right" but you don't say "switch right." Similarly, for the words *cat* and *lion*, you can find similar contexts, such as "A cat is a feline" and "A lion is a feline," but there are also contexts that are not so interchangeable for both words, such as "The cat lives in the city" and "The lion lives in the savanna."

The solution to this problem of mapping the one-hot representation of words into a more compact representation that preserves the notion of semantic distance has been solved in different ways in the past using classical statistics.[18] More recently neural networks provided a powerful solution in different forms, such as CBOW (Continuous Bag of Words) and SkipGrams.[19] Basically those solutions rely on training neural networks to predict words given a context. They have one-hot representation for both the input layer (i.e., the context) and the output layer (i.e., the word to predict), and a number of hidden neurons smaller than the vocabulary size. Once the network is trained on a large number of words and contexts, the vector of values corresponding to the activation of the hidden neurons is used as the representation for each word, and commonly called a *word embedding*. Word embeddings can be trained independently and can be reused for different systems to provide an effective coding of words that represents their semantic similarity relationship. Today we can also do multilingual embeddings that are able to code, in the same representation, words belonging to different languages.[20] By using multilingual embeddings, words of different languages that are semantically similar are close to each other in the embedding space. One advantage of using multilingual embeddings is that languages for which we do not have much training data can benefit from the NLU training of languages with large amounts of data.

NLU in Virtual Assistants

As opposed to the telephone-based virtual agents that prompt the user at each conversational turn, modern virtual AI assistants are always in an idle state expecting for a user to wake them up with a conventional phrase such as "Hey Google" or by pushing a button on a mobile telephone, and then issuing a request. In other words, the users initiate the interaction, and since they are not prompted, they can ask pretty much anything. In a very few cases, after a successful interaction, users are prompted to follow up with more information, as in the following example:

User: Hey Google set an alarm.

Assistant: Okay, when for?

User: 7:30 am.

Assistant: All right, the alarm is set for tomorrow at 7:30 am.

Because the assistant can expect pretty much anything when it is in its idle state, the NLU module faces a much higher complexity than the old telephone virtual agents had to handle. If NLU is based on grammars, all the grammars for all the allowed intents need to parse the transcription of the input utterance simultaneously to determine what the requested intent is. This operation, often referred to as *intent triggering*, raises a lot of technological issues since some requests may be intrinsically ambiguous. In that case, the ambiguity needs to be resolved at later stages of processing. For example, as we will see, the dialog manager may explicitly ask the user a clarification question, use the context to determine what the most likely interpretation is, or try to fulfill the request based on the different hypotheses and accept the one it considers the best result.

Data and Privacy

At present there is a tension in the development of NLU for commercial virtual assistants between using traditional handcrafted grammars including robust parsers, and applying machine learning data-driven methods. This tension exists for other components of virtual assistants as well, such as the natural language generator and the dialog manager, due to the fact that handcrafted methods still present some advantages over machine learning methods. The advantage is in their immediate availability. When designing an NLU system—for instance, to handle a feature of a virtual assistant—using an ML learning method requires the collection of a supervised training set of requests specific to that particular feature. That is not easy to do if the feature does not exist yet. And if the feature exists in some other forms, there may be privacy considerations that prevent the use of the system logs. At the same time, creating a grammar or a robust parser could be done quite easily by compiling a number of rules, often with the help of linguists, that would cover at least the most common requests.

Obviously a handcrafted NLU once deployed will not perform optimally. Even though the linguists that have crafted the grammar may have foreseen all the possible ways to request a particular service, they may not have predicted the whole variety of unexpected utterances that still make sense. Remember, as we noticed earlier, that in a modern virtual assistants users are not prompted or guided on what to say, but rather can say pretty much anything, making it hard to create grammars that can cover all the possible utterances.

Once a system is deployed, one could use the transcripts of the sessions, the so called *logs*, to improve the grammars or train ML-based NLUs. However, user privacy concerns impose constraints on accessing the user logs. Those constraints need to be taken into utmost consideration. As a minimum, in no circumstance should the developers of a virtual assistant be able to identify the user of a given utterance, or any associated private information. Today the general public is becoming increasingly aware of the risks posed to privacy by today's digital world, including social networks, home devices, and virtual assistants. Lawmakers in many countries are taking action to regulate the handling of private data in order to protect their citizens. One example is GDPR, the General Data Protection Regulation enacted by the European Parliament and the Council of the European Union in 2016. GDPR imposed changes on data handling processes that prompted the industry to make changes to its existing platforms in order to comply. Research is moving in a direction where amassing personal data is becoming less important for the improvement of ML-based technology, such as speech recognition and natural language understanding. Increasing emphasis is on unsupervised learning, synthetic data, and techniques that process data on the user device, such as a smartphone or a home device, and do not require uploading user data to the cloud.

Federated learning developed by Google is an example of that. Federated learning, used today for improving speech recognition and text processing by correcting errors on a mobile soft keyboard, is based on decentralized learning and aggregation. With federated learning the user's speech or text never leaves their phone and is used to improve the local performance of the technology in question—for example, speech recognition dictation—by ML training that takes place on the device itself. This is made possible by the increasingly powerful computing resources available on personal devices such as phones and tablets. While the private data never leaves the user device, the results of the on-device-trained DNNs can occasionally be uploaded to the cloud, in a secure encrypted form, and aggregated with the results of all the users, in order to improve the general accuracy of the technology in question. That is the concept of federation: a centralized control that allows for independent learning by the individual agents, but still gains from the accumulated knowledge. It is important to note that there is no way to recover the original data from the encrypted results of a neural network, since the results consist of just the parameters of individual neurons aggregated over the course of many iterations of backpropagation learning. In this way the user data is secure on the user device, and the ML models can gain from learning from millions of users.

NLU Today

If we were to qualitatively rate the performance of today's NLU systems in virtual assistants we would probably realize that they are not as advanced as we would like. It is not infrequent to encounter situations where the speech recognizer returns the correct transcription of an utterance into words, but the NLU module does not understand its meaning and consequently does not trigger the correct action. When you invoke an assistant, such as Siri or the Google Assistant, from a mobile phone by asking a question, it is not infrequent for the screen to display web search results rather than a correct answer to your specific query. This is how the assistant hedges when it does not understand the query. Posting the web information is the assistant's way of admitting, "I don't know what you are talking about, but here is a web search done with the words you told me." Next generations of virtual assistants must be developed with the capacity to understand the meaning of more and more queries, in order to provide specific answers without falling back on web search results.

One of the reasons why NLU technology today is not yet as advanced and accurate as we would expect is that although ML can effectively learn to transform textual queries into intents and arguments, there is still a lot of heavy handcrafting needed to build a complete and effective NLU system. While we could collect large amounts of transcribed utterances in order to properly use today's supervised ML, we would still have to annotate each of them with the right intent and arguments.[21] That's a process that requires intensive labor by human annotators highly trained on the specific domain. It also is quite error prone, since there may be instances of vague utterances whose association to a certain intent may not be clear. It is also not easy to build tools that will enable human annotators to select one intent out of thousands for a given utterance transcription. And some of the intents in the list may be very similar and hard to distinguish from one another. In other words, the annotation of data for NLU is poorly scalable.

In contrast, compare the annotation of NLU data with that of the data needed to train an ASR. Classic ASR recognizes words by relying on their phonetic models. Those models are created by assigning fixed phonetic base forms to words. The human annotators need only transcribe each utterance into the sequence of spoken words in their orthographic form. The training required for human annotators is minimal and to a certain extent anyone who is proficient in the language in use can transcribe utterances into the corresponding words. That means that for speech recognition it is easy to obtain large amounts of speech data labeled with the correct words and thus train better and better models. However, as noted previously, with the increased awareness of the right to user privacy, a growing number of techniques are being deployed that do not require data labeled by human annotators.[22]

The situation is totally different for NLU. There is not an existing, universal, consolidated set of intents that can be used to map any possible utterance into their meaning. So, for every system, the intent structure has to be crafted by hand, and the human annotators have to understand each utterance, know the intent structure, and assign the correct intent. That's a lot of specialized work that is costly and hard to scale to the proportion required by a virtual assistant. Because of that, data for NLU training is not abundant and every new domain requires laborious crafting of the intent structure and a laborious annotation process. Consistency and universality of the intent structure is hard to achieve across different organizations, even within the same company. That's one of the reasons why the progress of NLU systems has been slower than, for instance, the progress of speech recognition.

NATURAL LANGUAGE AND SPEECH GENERATION

While the job of the ASR and NLU components is to understand spoken human language, the job of natural language generation (NLG) and text-to-speech (TTS) is to speak back to the user.

There is a reverse analogy between the input channel, corresponding to the ASR and NLU, and the output channel represented by the NLG and TTS. For the input channel the ASR takes speech as input and generates text to feed the NLU, which in turn generates a symbolic representation of its meaning. The output channel starts at the other end. The NLG is activated by a symbolic request of what the virtual assistant needs to say, and generates a textual representation of it. The TTS system then transforms that text into actual speech. Let's start by looking at the NLG.

Research scientists have been working on natural language generation for decades. In principle the goal is

The NLG is activated by a symbolic request of what the virtual assistant needs to say, and generates a textual representation of it. The TTS system then transforms that text into actual speech.

a system that does the exact opposite of what NLU does, that is, it takes a symbolic representation of meaning as input and generates a grammatical and natural textual sentence as output. One of the traditional approaches is to generate language based on a sequence of modules. The first module is a *planner* that creates the high-level structure of the sentence, followed by a *microplanner* that creates the structure of the segments, or phrases, and finally a *lexicalizer* that chooses the words for the final realization and refinement of the sentence.[1]

Nowadays the NLG module of many commercial virtual assistants needs to balance the expressivity, naturalness, and control that are not always available with the most sophisticated methods based on neural networks. As a matter of fact, in its simplest version NLG can be realized with a repository of textual sentences (often called *prompts*) indexed so they can be easily retrieved by the dialog manager when needed. Indeed, for most of the early virtual agents, the telephone IVR systems, each prompt was actually a file of speech recorded by a professional voice talent, thus encompassing both the language and speech generation phases.

Prerecorded prompts would work well today for relatively simple systems that require only a set of static responses fully specified at design time. For more complex systems, some of the output prompts may need to have variable content. Imagine a virtual assistant that would have to speak the predicted arrival time of a flight, such as

Flight 56 is landing in New York JFK at six thirty-five pm.

Prerecording all the possible combinations of flight numbers, times, and arrival airports would result in a large number of audio files. The cost and the time needed for recording all of them would be impractical. Besides, if new combinations of flight number, time, and arrival airport are introduced, one would need to record new prompts. Early on, before text-to-speech systems were able to produce high-quality synthetic voices, IVR systems used a technique called CPR (concatenative prompt recording). The selected voice talent was coached to record all of the segments that could be used to assemble all the possible prompts and their variations. For the preceding examples, the talent would record the following segments:

flight

is landing in

at

In addition to that, the voice talent would record all the individual digits and number fragments, like *thirty*, *forty* and so on, the words *am* and *pm*, and all the airport names (the number of airport names is large but not infinite). At runtime a special module would fetch the segments required to assemble variable prompts and splice them in the right order. To ensure the resulting assembled speech sounded natural, special care was to be taken in recording the segments and in their splicing. In particular, the collection of segments included different versions with different intonations to account for the position in the sentence where the segment would appear—beginning, middle, or end—so that the final intonation would sound natural. That technique accounted for both NLG and TTS in a single module, and addressed the fact that the quality of TTS at that time was not high enough to be acceptable in a commercial application.

Template-Based NLG

Since modern TTS voice synthesis systems can speak any textual sentences with a high-quality voice that is often indistinguishable from human recordings, there is no need to splice large numbers of accurately recorded segments to generate prompts. Whatever a modern assistant speaks is created as text by a proper NLG system, and then sent to a generic TTS to generate the required output utterance.

In commercial systems there is still substantial handcrafting in the generation of the output responses. One of the most common techniques consists in using textual templates like the following:[2]

> Flight $flight-number is landing at $airport-name at $time.

The constant portions of the template in this example are represented by textual words, and the variable parts by symbols that are indicated as variable names preceded by the $ sign.[3] The variable parts will be substituted, at runtime, for the proper values by the NLG system. The final text is then sent to the TTS to speak the full sentence out.

Of course this is a basic example, but in real systems there might be more complicated situations. For instance, a response prompt may have to handle singular and plural words. If the prompt is a response to questions like "How long before my warranty expires?," the virtual assistant will have to use the singular or plural for the word *year* depending on the answer (e.g., *one year* vs. *two years*).

Besides number agreement, and gender and case agreement for languages such as Italian or French, there could be other conditions that should be used to construct the right sentence and that can depend on the context. An opening prompt could start with "Good morning," "Good afternoon," or "Good evening," depending on the time of the day. In addition, depending on the application, language, and cultural environment, the style of the prompt may be different based on the user's gender, age, and level of familiarity with the system. Furthermore, depending on the sentiment of the message to be delivered, the text, and even the final intonation of the speech, may be different.

Other interesting variations of the output messages may depend on past interaction history. A technique called *prompt tapering* is often used to make a virtual assistant avoid repeating information that has been spoken earlier, thereby reducing the verbosity of subsequent prompts, as in the following example, where the prompts are successively less informative.

Assistant: What is the length of your package in inches? Please approximate to the nearest inch.

User: 25 inches.

Assistant: What is the width of your package in inches?

User: 10 inches.

Assistant: What its height?

User: 5 inches.

Notice that, in the above example, the approximation instruction is not repeated after the first prompt, and the third prompt does not repeat that the measure has to be in inches, assuming that the user has learned that information by then.

Finally, in order for the assistant to be pleasant and not annoyingly repetitive, one may want to use a different version of the same prompt at different times in a more or less random manner. For instance:

User: What is the weather like?

Assistant: Today is sunny with a high of 28. Dress lightly, it's going to be warm.

And if the user asks the same question again a short time later:

User: What's the weather today?

Assistant: Sunny with a high temperature of 28 degrees. Don't forget to take your sunglasses.

It is clear how even a simple template-based system for natural language generation can easily become a sophisticated tool that includes code to account for syntactical and stylistic variations of the messages spoken by the AI assistant. Yet, a full-fledged template-based NLG will provide a high level of control for the assistant designers and developers.

When the output sentences become more complex, the natural language generation system needs to make adjustments to the language in order for the sentences to sound natural. This happens when the user query includes more than one question, such as

When was Albert Einstein born, and where?

A simple answer would be

Albert Einstein was born on March 14, 1879. Albert Einstein was born in Ulm, Germany.

Of course, a more natural-speaking system would give a more concise answer, such as:

Albert Einstein was born in Ulm, Germany, on March 14, 1879.

That's because birthplace and date are closely related and naturally spoken in a single phrase. Other facts may require the use of conjunctions or prepositions:

When was Albert Einstein born, and when did he die?

Albert Einstein was born on March 14, 1879, and he died on April 18, 1955.

Finally, another interesting issue for natural language generation is summarization. Often a user may ask questions that require the assistant to speak a long list. Examples include weather forecasts for the next week or ten days; the daily schedule of appointments and meetings, and so on. Here is an example:

User: What is the weather for next week in New York?

Assistant: From this Sunday to next Saturday, in New York the low will be around 40 and the high around 52. From Wednesday to Friday it will be cloudy with chances of rain.

In this example, rather than giving a day-by-day weather forecast, the assistant summarizes the weather in a few sentences, a process called *aggregation* in linguistics. That requires an algorithm that groups the daily weather forecasts in similar multiday segments and expresses them in a way that is familiar to the user.

As in other modules of a virtual assistant, machine learning is starting to substitute handcrafted, rule-based, or template-based algorithms with data-driven modules.

Back to Speech

After the NLG determines *what to say* and expresses it in a textual form, the next step consists in the generation of the corresponding utterance. Traditionally that is called *text-to-speech* (or TTS). Even though TTS is conceptually the inverse functionality of a speech recognizer (which is often called speech-to-text), its technological issues are somewhat different, even though they both may use similar technologies.

TTS is a cascade of three distinct modules. The first, text normalization, makes the text readable by resolving words and phrases whose spoken form may not be obvious. We do that process in our mind when we read out loud. Even though we may think that text contains all the elements needed for us to read it correctly, that is not quite true. When we read out loud we implicitly use a lot of rules and conventions. Read, for example, the following paragraph:[4]

> Yesterday I went to the bank at the corner of St. James St. to deposit a check for 1983 dollars. I remember when in 1997 I went to the same bank to deposit my first paycheck of $300. The date was 5/25 and that amount was 1/10 of my salary today. As I reached the office, the teller gave me a piece of paper to read. I read it and it said . . .

No one would have any problem reading that, but think about the many issues that a reading machine would have to deal with. To start, the abbreviation "St." is read as "Saint" in its first occurrence, and then as "Street." The number "1983" is read as "one thousand nine hundred and eighty three" because it is clearly interpreted as an amount, but the number "1997" is read as "nineteen ninety seven" because it indicates a year, as it is obvious from the context, and that's how we speak years in English. "$300" is read as "three hundred dollars" and not "dollars three hundred" as would be otherwise suggested by the "$" symbol coming before the number. And "5/25," clearly a date, is read as "five twenty five"—or "May twenty fifth" if you will—while "1/10" is read as "one tenth" because, although it could be a date, it is instead a numerical fraction as the context suggests. Then, the first occurrence of the word *read* is pronounced differently than the second because the second one is in past tense. Clearly, there are many decisions we have to make when we read based on context and interpretation. A computer transforming text to speech needs to be able to make the same decisions in the text normalization phase.

TTS systems also need to take punctuation into proper account. Punctuation, like periods, commas, colons, and semicolons indicate how to break text into phrases and sentences, and how to read text with the proper pauses and intonation. Questions and exclamation marks are often expressed in different languages by different intonations, like raising or falling vocal pitch. Punctuation is also important to resolve ambiguous phrases and sentences. For instance, "The panda eats shoots and leaves" has a totally different meaning than "The panda eats, shoots, and leaves."[5]

However, punctuation symbols and their relationship with sentences and phrases are not obvious at all. Periods are used not only to terminate sentences, but also to indicate decimal points in numbers (1.34) and dates (1.25.2010) and commas are used to indicate thousands ($1,200). And that usage changes from language to language: in several European countries, for example, the period sign is used to separate thousands in a large number, and the comma is used to indicate decimals, as in 1.200.325,45, while its use is just the opposite in the United States. Periods are also used to terminate abbreviations, like in "etc.," and sometimes to separate the characters in some acronyms, like "e.g." and "i.e." And if a sentence ends with an abbreviation, just one period is often used to indicate both the end of the abbreviation, and the end of the sentence.

Numbers are clearly another problem for text-to-speech. As we saw in the previous example numbers are read differently depending on whether they indicate a date, a year, a quantity, a telephone number, or the model of an object, such as a "747 airplane." Roman ordinals have similar issues, like in "Chapter III" (chapter three) and "Henry III" (Henry the third). We saw the problem with abbreviations: "St." and "Dr." can be streets or saints, doctors or drives. Acronyms are sometimes pronounced letter by letter, as in IBM, or as single words, as in NATO, or AIDS. These and many other problems make the task of text preprocessing very complex and language dependent. Each language has special reading rules that need to be coded as part of the text normalization module.

Phonetic transcription follows the normalization module, and transforms the normalized text into a sequence of symbols representing the sounds of that language, generally called *phonemes*.[6] As you may recall we encountered a similar problem in speech recognition when we discussed how to build models of words. However, going from the orthographic representation of a word to its phonetics for any possible word of a text can be very complex. In particular, for languages such as English, which has very irregular pronunciation, rules are often contradictory, and some words are written in the same way but are spoken differently depending on the context, their meaning or syntactic use.[7] The word *read*, as we saw, changes its pronunciation when used as the past tense of the verb *to read*, and stress on the word *conduct* is placed on a different syllable depending on whether it is a noun or a verb. Thus a program to automatically assign the correct sequence of phonemes to any string of text needs to take into consideration a set of general pronunciation rules, a large list of exceptions, as well as the actual syntax of the phrases or sentences that have to be spoken, and the part of speech represented by each word in the input text. And of course we won't even mention the difficulties presented by other languages, such as Arabic, where the correct vowels typically are not even written but need to be inferred from the context; or Chinese and Japanese, where the correspondence between characters and sounds is not straightforward at all. All of these variabilities have to be taken into account by the phonetic transcription module. Word juncture is another source of complexity for the phonetic transcriber. Coarticulation phenomena need to be considered since the pronunciation of the initial or final parts of each word may be affected by the preceding or following word, and this is true not only for English, but also for other languages as well.

However, providing a correct phonetic transcription is only half the job. When we speak in a natural way we introduce *intonation*. Intonation not only is important for making the voice sound natural, as opposed to robotic, but it also carries additional information about the meaning of a sentence. By changing loudness, pitch, and duration during the pronunciation of an utterance we may put the stress on one of the words to convey a special meaning. "I did the work" may convey a different meaning if the stress is on the word *I* (meaning "I did the work, not you!") or on the word *work* (meaning "The work is done, and I did it"). By changing the pitch we can make an utterance sound like a question or as a statement, as in "You?" vs. "You!" even though the phrase, in this case one word, may not be grammatically formed to be a question or a statement. Moreover, we can express sarcasm, kindness, surprise, or urgency, by changing the intonation of an utterance. Try saying "OK" with different intonations and see how many different subtle meanings you can express.

Intonation is expressed by controlling three fundamental properties of speech: pitch, loudness, and duration. TTS systems model those three parameters to follow a number of natural intonation patterns along an utterance. Some TTS systems let the designer and engineer who use them change the parameters that control intonation by adding special symbols in the text.

The next, final step is the actual production of the speech signal starting from the normalized text, its transcription into the correct sounds, and the parameters required to produce the desired intonation. The actual production of a speech signal is performed by a module known as the speech synthesizer, or *vocoder*.

The history of speech synthesis is older than that of speech recognition. We know of several attempts to reproduce the human voice mechanically, dating back to the eighteenth century, some of them quite successful.[8] However, the first speech synthesizer of the modern era was designed and built at Bell Laboratories by scientist Homer Dudley, and demonstrated to the public at the New York World's Fair in 1939. The text preprocessing and the phonetic transcription functions were performed by a human operator sitting at a keyboard who was trained to translate sentences into sequences of phonemes. Then the operator typed the right keys corresponding to those phonemes on the keyboard of Dudley's invention, called the Voder, while controlling the pitch and vocalization of the sounds with levers. The machine could then speak with a robotic but somewhat intelligible voice.

After the introduction of digital computers, speech synthesis evolved in different ways. Initially, handcrafted rules governed the spectral patterns of speech sounds; later, speech was synthesized by concatenating parametric models of phonemes; and finally, in the early 2000s, snippets of waveforms of phonetic sounds, words, and phrases were selected from a large collection and spliced one after the other to achieve the most natural utterances. This last was called *concatenative,* or *corpus-based synthesis*, and it produced an impressively human-like quality provided that the inventory of snippets was large enough.

Speech synthesis based on Hidden Markov Models, developed after corpus-based synthesis, generated even higher quality speech, and most recently, the use of DNNs has brought us synthetic speech that is almost indistinguishable from human speech. In 2015 Google acquired the company DeepMind, which develops innovative applications of deep learning. In particular, one of its products, WaveNet, is based on a novel technique for generating audio and speech based on convolutional neural networks.[9] The result is practically indistinguishable from human speech. Initially WaveNet required several minutes of computation to generate a single waveform, but after a lot of architectural and algorithmic improvements it could synthesize speech at a rate that is a fraction of the duration of the utterance, and it is currently used as the voice of the Google Assistant and other Google products.

THE DIALOG MANAGER

The dialog manager (DM) is at the heart, or better the brain, of a virtual assistant. The main function of a dialog manager is to decide the next action that the assistant should perform, based on the current input from the user, the history, or *context*, of the conversation, the status of the outside world, or *the environment*, and a specification of how the assistant would behave in different and specific situations. That is called a *strategy* or *policy*.

Similar to the other modules of a virtual assistant, there is an abundant amount of research work being done on dialog management. The systems built in the ARPA SUR program of the 1970s projects discussed earlier, notably HARPY, had some built-in dialog management. Right after the ATIS project that ended in 1994, DARPA followed up with a new project that focused on dialog based on the same airline information domain and revolving around a common architecture. The project was called the DARPA Communicator.[1] At the same time, at the end of the 1990s, European labs and industry contributed to development of dialog management technology with projects and novel architectures.[2]

Instructing the NLG system to say something, such as a response to a query, is one of the actions that the dialog manager performs based on the current user input and context. In some cases the dialog manager responds to the user directly, or searches the internet, to get additional information necessary for the requested task. For instance, imagine the user asks: "What's the weather?" In order to answer this question, the dialog manager first needs to determine where the user is located geographically, then query an external weather service, then collect the response and format it according to a specific established protocol for the NLG system to speak it out. If the assistant is not a voice-only system but also has a display, the dialog manager also needs to create a visual output. In this example, assume that the location of the user is readily available to the dialog manager. For example, the user may have registered her location in a setup phase, or notified the assistant about that earlier, or the location could be readily available because the user is interacting with a device that has GPS enabled (a smartphone, for example), or location is estimated from the device's internet address (which is the most common case for devices like desktops that do not have GPS). But there might be a situation where none of the above applies. If the user location is not readily available, in order to fulfill the user's request the dialog manager would have to ask the user directly: "Where are you located?" That would result in an additional conversational turn. Assuming that the user responds with a known location, for instance "New York," the DM would use that to query the weather service and provide the correct answer.

What if something goes wrong? What if when the user is asked for her location, she does not answer, or she answers with something that is not a location? Or what if the ASR confuses one word with another? Here is an example of a user interaction where just about everything that can go wrong does:

User: What's the . . . weather?

ASR returns "<u>What's the</u>" since the last part of the utterance is cut after the long pause.

Assistant: Sorry, what was that?

User: I want to know what the weather is.

Assistant: OK. Weather. For where?

[User is silent for a while]

Assistant: Sorry, you want to hear the weather for where?

User: New York.

Assistant: Today in Newark, NJ, is sunny with a high of 68.

User: No, I said NEW YORK.

Assistant: Sure. Today in New York, NY, is sunny with a high of 70.

Of course, this example is a little contrived, but all of the problems it presents may actually happen in a speech recognition–based system. A well-designed dialog manager needs to be able to handle the range of problems that can occur in a spoken interaction. Early dialog manager techniques, developed initially for telephone customer-care applications, took care of those situations by using configurable dialog modules that had well-defined and reusable reprompting strategies in case something went wrong such as the user failing to respond to a prompt, called a user timeout, and speech recognition errors.[3]

When we talk naturally we assume that listeners not only are aware of what we're telling them now, but also of what we said before, as well as the general *context* of the conversation, including its purpose and location. Context is extremely important in determining the meaning of what we say. Certain expressions have a meaning only in certain contexts, and no meaning in others. Imagine stopping a stranger in the street and telling him, "Two pounds of ground meat." In the best possible scenario, the stranger would look at you, puzzled, and ask you what you mean. More likely, he'd think you were very weird and wouldn't answer. But if you say the same thing to the employee standing behind the counter at the meat department of your supermarket, that would be perfectly OK. The employee would smile and give you what you requested. Similarly, in another context, the answer to the question "Who is his wife?" depends on who we were just talking about. Or even more subtle, if I talk about "python," I mean the snake or the homonymous computer language, depending on whether I'm talking about my latest visit to the zoo, or my programming skills.

The knowledge of our personal context, as users of a virtual assistant, assumes an increasingly important role in the interpretation of our queries, and can make the conversation more natural and effective. Imagine you are in London and ask your virtual assistant, "How long does it take to get to the airport?" There are six airports servicing London—which one of them? If the assistant knows the context, that you are expected to board your next flight in a few hours from the airport of Gatwick, it will give you the right information and avoid asking you a question for which it already has the answer. Imagine if you interact with a human assistant, and he asks you those clarifying questions all the time, when if he just learned a little bit more about you he wouldn't have to. After a while you'll probably get irritated and you may even consider firing him, because after all he is not very useful.

Let's go back now to the most obvious context constituted by the previous interactions with the assistant. Imagine you asked your assistant, "When was Barack Obama president of the United States?" The assistant gives you the correct answer: "Barack Obama served from the 20th of January 2009 to the 20th of January 2017." Then you want to follow up with more questions about President Obama. In normal, natural conversations between humans you would not repeat the subject "Barack Obama" since you have set a clear context with your first question. You would say, "How old is he? How old is his wife? Who are his children?" In this particular example we normally use what is called a pronominal reference, where the pronouns "he" and "his" are used to refer directly to the object of the previous query, meaning Barack Obama. But in a slightly more complex query we may actually use a pronoun to refer to the result of the previous query, rather than the previous query itself, as in the following exchange:

User: What is the tallest building in the world?

Assistant: Burj Khalifa, 2,720 feet tall, is the tallest building in the world.

User: Where is it?

The knowledge of our personal context, as users of a virtual assistant, assumes an increasingly important role in the interpretation of our queries, and can make the conversation more natural and effective.

Assistant: In Dubai.

User: How far is it from here?

Assistant: Dubai is 6,836 miles from here.

In this example, the first use of the pronoun *it* ("Where is it?") refers to Burj Khalifa, which was mentioned in the answer, while the second is ambiguous and could refer either to Dubai or Burj Khalifa. In this case the assistant decided to use the latest reference—Dubai.

Sometimes we don't even use full sentences but incomplete phrases to indicate we want to change just the specific subject for the request we spoke earlier, such as in the second user query of the following interaction:

User: What's the weather in New York?

Assistant: The weather in New York is . . .

User: What about Boston?

Assistant: The weather in Boston is . . .

User: And the temperature?

Assistant: The temperature in Boston is . . .

User: Baltimore?

Assistant: Today it's 72 degrees in Baltimore.

It's clear that a proper virtual assistant should be able to handle all of those linguistic references. Imagine if every time we asked something that referred to previous interactions we had to repeat all the requests verbatim. That would be cumbersome, stilted, and unnatural. The preceding conversation would have to take this form:

User: What's the weather in New York?

Assistant: The weather in New York is . . .

User: What is the weather in Boston?

Assistant: The weather in Boston is . . .

User: What is the temperature in Boston?

Assistant: The temperature in Boston is . . .

Modern assistants are able to manage referential pronouns and incomplete sentences (called elliptical sentences) based on algorithms that unravel the structure of each query, determine whether the query is incomplete and missing elements such as the specific subject or intent, and try to answer it by resolving the missing elements with the right information. Those algorithms are based on a mix of language rules and the results of data analysis on large corpora of queries done in the past and aggregated over all the users. When the assistant employs a visual display, like on a smartphone or a home screen device, what is displayed is also part of the context to be addressed. Imagine at a certain point you have a picture of an actress on your screen and you want to ask, "What is her latest movie?" Or you see one of the photos you've taken with your phone, and you want to know, "Where was this photo taken?" Or imagine a song is playing on your smart speaker at home, and you ask, "Who is singing this song?" Modern technology allows you to ask this question, and in most cases you will get the correct answer from your device.

Another function that a dialog manager should be able to handle is the proper resolution of ambiguities. Homonyms and homophones—words that are spelled or pronounced in the same way but refer to different entities or different meanings—are among the most common sources of ambiguities. In certain languages, proper names often have one or more homophones. If I ask my assistant to "call Jon," the ASR may process that input as "call John," because the pronunciation of John and Jon are the same, and there is no way for the speech recognizer to distinguish between the two. It's the same for Alan vs. Allen vs. Allan, who could be different people among my contacts who spell their name in different ways.

Some of these homophones can be resolved based on the linguistic context, and the speech recognizer alone is able to resolve that without using additional information, relying on a bias introduced by a personalized language model. If in the past I've called Jon more often than John, the dialog manager can use that knowledge to interpret the name returned by the ASR as Jon, and not John. However, if I actually want to call John, and not my usual choice of Jon, the assistant may make a mistake that I will have to correct, perhaps by speaking the full name of the person I want to call in order to give the ASR more context to produce the right result. However, since I call Jon more often than John, that mistake would not happen that often. But if I call both Jon and John roughly with the same frequency, any decision may be wrong 50 percent of the time. And what if I have many Jons and many Johns in my contact list? In those situations, the dialog manager should ask clarification questions to determine which Jo(h)n to call, and retain that data to speed up the interaction next time. All of these considerations are relevant in designing a dialog manager. An important criterion for the design of a dialog manager is to make interactions faster, including reducing the number of turns in an interaction by favoring more frequent interpretations in ambiguous cases.[4]

But there are other types of ambiguities that may require the dialog manager to resolve them. For example, you may ask your assistant to play a song, but as we know, there may be many versions of that song sung by the same or different artists. Or you may ask the assistant to set an alarm for seven o'clock, and the assistant needs to determine whether you mean am or pm. And if you have several alarms set and you ask the assistant to "cancel the alarm" it will have to figure out which of the many alarms you set you want to cancel. If your device has a display, the assistant can show you a list of the alarms you have set, and you can click or speak the one you want to cancel (e.g., "the third alarm in the list"). Again, the assistant needs to be aware of the display's context to select the proper element in the list: the third one.

In addition to handling functions such as these, and their related issues, the dialog manager is the interface between the user and the rest of the world. As such it needs to fulfill any user request whenever possible. To do so, the dialog manager needs to interact with external systems of the digital world, query or control them, and interpret their responses. These external systems may have different functions, including:

• Provide answers to general knowledge queries—such as "How old is Barack Obama?"—using generic search engines or repositories such as Wikipedia.

• Provide answers to questions directed to the virtual assistant itself, such as "How old are you?" "What is your favorite animal?" "What is the meaning of life?" The answers are specifically tailored to the assistant and its personality.

- Deliver jokes, games, other entertaining content.

- Provide the user's personal information in response to questions like these: "When is my flight to London leaving?" or "When is my next dentist appointment?"

- Play public or personal media content upon request, such as music, videos, photos, or films, depending on device capabilities.

- Interact with the external *analog* world with devices connected to the internet, such as home automation devices, and perform operations such as "Switch the lights in the dining room on" or "Unlock the back door."

To summarize, stripped down to its basic functionality, the only responsibility of a dialog manager is to determine what the system will do next and execute it or delegate it to another system. That does not mean, necessarily, that the DM is responsible for providing the correct answer to a question (e.g., "How old is Barack Obama?") or performing the requested action (e.g., "Set an alarm for 7:30 am"). Rather, the DM is responsible for deciding which system can provide the right answer or perform the requested action, then invoke it with the right protocol, and return an answer or an acknowledgment back to the user. In the process, the DM is also responsible for determining whether the user request contains all the information necessary for its fulfillment, and asking for any missing information.

Dialog Manager Architecture

What a dialog manager does may seem simple enough, to the point that a software developer can write a program with a lot of IF-THEN-ELSE rules to do exactly that. And, indeed, that's often the case for simple systems. But when systems start to become complex, with a lot of possibilities, and a lot of exceptions, merely writing IF-THEN-ELSE computer programs may not guarantee scalability toward increasingly sophisticated capabilities, and maintainability can become an issue. In fact, how to build an effective dialog manager is still open to debate, and there is not an obvious, established solution.

While dialog systems driven by machine learning and user data may be a solution in the longer term, and research is actively looking into that, sophisticated AI assistants may still resort to manual handcrafting of rule-based systems, and tools that are designed to allow easy development and maintenance of complex dialog managers. Some of them also use large amounts of data to infer some of the rules and thus reduce the need to handcraft them, at least for some dialog management functions.

One of the leading paradigms for dialog managers is based on the definition of its behavior—the dialog policy, or strategy—as a finite state machine, or FSM, controller. That came about in the 1990s when touch-tone IVR applications (press 1 for this, 2 for that, etc.) became a popular way to automate services, and their complexity grew to the point that they needed a clear and structured design and development paradigm. The most popular design paradigm turned out to be FSMs. When the industry moved from DTMF touch-tone-based to voice recognition–based systems, the industry extended the FSM-based paradigm to voice as well.

A basic FSM dialog manager is defined by a number of states and the transitions among them. Any state represents a particular turn of the interaction. The transitions out of each state are associated with conditions, typically based on what the user said, or other pieces of information that would cause the interaction to move to a different state. Consider this example: as soon as a user starts interacting with an FSM-based customer care assistant, the FSM is in an initial state, the *welcome* state, in which the assistant greets the user and provides instructions on how to proceed (see figure 5). Immediately after the welcome state, the system would prompt the user to make a choice, for instance:

How can I help you? Please say: account information, technical support, or billing.

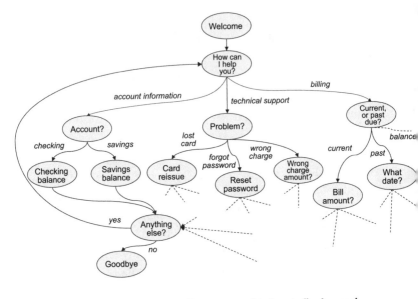

Figure 5 Example of an FSM (finite state machine) controller for a goal-oriented dialog system.

For this interaction, the welcome state requires at least three transitions: one for "account information," one for "technical support," and one for "billing." An additional transition is needed to address the possibility of a "no-match," which occurs when the user's request *does not match* what is expected by the dialog system, and consequently by the underlying grammar. There also has to be a *timeout* transition, if the user does not say anything for a specific amount of time (e.g., for a few seconds).

And finally, there should be a transition to account for a user asking the assistant to "repeat" the initial message (that transition would go back to the initial state), and one for the user asking for "help." To avoid clutter, figure 5 does not show the no-match, timeout, repeat, and help transitions, but you can assume they are available for every state, since these four situations can happen at any point in the interaction.[5] We'll talk about them in a minute.

A total of seven transitions out of the welcome state lead to the corresponding next states. Each next state will then have other transitions, and so on. For instance, if the user says "billing," the dialog manager would go into a state called "Current, or past, due?" (notice that this is simply the name of the state, and not what the assistant will speak out) that may ask the user:

> Billing. Pay a current bill? Pay a past due bill? Or get your balance?

And here too there will be three transitions to a corresponding number of states, plus four additional transitions for no-match, timeout, repeat, and help.

Let's imagine that, on average, an interaction would require five turns to reach completion, corresponding to five levels of menus. The transitions from the first state, in our example, would lead to seven states, each of which would lead to seven other states, and so on. In total we will have a number of states and corresponding transitions of the order of 7 to the power of 5, that is, 16,807 states. Depending on the problem, an interaction may need more than five turns, so you can imagine how quickly the number of states will become unmanageable.

One of the first of the industry's innovations was based on the realization that most of the states share nearly the same logic, which can be expressed as follows:

a) Play the initial prompt, often called the "collection" prompt.

b) Activate the speech recognizer with a defined grammar.

c) Wait for the user's speech. One of the following may happen:

    i) The user says something that matches one of the possible options (and the corresponding grammar) → go to the next state.

    ii) The user says something that does not match anything → play a *no-match* prompt, activate the speech recognizer, and go back to b), unless the number of no-matches that happened before in this state is higher than a defined maximum value, in which case exit with an error condition.

iii) The user does not say anything for a determined amount of time. → play a *timeout* prompt, activate the speech recognizer, and go back to b) unless the number of timeouts that happened before in this state is higher than a defined maximum value, in which case exit with an error condition.

iv) The user asks for additional help → play a help prompt, activate the speech recognizer, and go back to b) unless the number of help requests that happened before in this state is higher than a defined maximum value, in which case exit with an error condition.

v) The user asks to repeat the request → repeat the initial prompt, and go back to b) unless the number of repeat requests that happened before in this state is higher than a defined maximum value, in which case exit with an error condition.

The idea of codifying this general behavior evolved in what came to be known as *dialog modules*. Dialog modules with the general built-in logic previously described were the building blocks of complex dialog applications. Dialog modules are configurable by specifying the actual prompts, grammars, maximum number of no-matches, and time-outs. To create an interaction, a designer would specify the states and transitions of the FSM, and the configuration of the dialog modules associated with each state. Each dialog module requires the specification of the prompts, in other words the collection, no-match, timeout, and help prompts, and the grammar for the speech recognizer to collect and understand the most common expressions that users would say when exposed to those prompts. Configurable specialized dialog modules were also made available for the collection of information that would recur often in typical applications, such as dates and times of various formats, amounts of money in different currencies, credit card numbers, and so on. The configurable dialog modules were very helpful for designers and developers to streamline the lifecycle of complex dialog systems.

Yet, even with this simplification, a complex application would still require a large number of dialog modules connected with conditional transitions to form a quite intricate graph.

Building a virtual agent for customer care required at least two types of skilled professionals: conversation designers and software engineers. The conversation (or voice user interface, or VUI) designer would design the full dialog interaction, in the form of a complex graph (an FSM as discussed above), with dialog modules and their configuration, and the conditional transitions among them. The VUI designers would pass their design on to the software engineers, who would then write a computer program to implement the FSM with dialog models and thus implement the design.

Some companies found a better way to approach the two step (design + software implementation) process. After all, the programmer's job is to replicate the design in computer software. By making sure that the code and the design representation are based on analogous structures, companies like SpeechCycle built tools that would automatically translate a design done on a graphical design tool directly and automatically into software, thus eliminating one step of the process. VUI designers could use the graphical design tool to build dialog graphs similar to the one in figure 5 and configure them, still using the tool. The graphical tool would then convert the design into software that could run on the server, and the designers could test their creation immediately and make any necessary changes.

Of course, building a large FMS with hundreds of states and thousands of transitions would be daunting, even with the support of a graphical tool. However, the engineers who built those tools allowed the designers to use the same abstractions that programmers use to make software manageable, such as the use of hierarchical recursion (a state of an FSM can be an FSM as well) and inheritance (a state could inherit its properties from another state). Those abstractions would help make large FSMs manageable. Using a tool like that SpeechCycle could build sophisticated dialog systems that would engage users in dozens of turns for several minutes, and help them solve issues with their internet or cable TV at home.

Interjections

So far we have discussed interactions in which the system prompts the user and the user responds according to what is prompted for—directed dialog. This is typical of customer-care virtual agents, and can be well represented by FSMs. However, even in directed dialog, there are situations where FSMs seem to be inadequate, or hard to scale. That is the case with user interjections. An interjection in a conversation happens when one of the parties, in our case the user, momentarily deviates from her course and asks a nonrelated, or slightly related, question. For instance:

Assistant: Billing. What do you want to do? Pay a current bill? Pay a past-due bill? Or get your balance?

User: How much money do I have in my checking account?

Of course, the user utterance, like many other possible questions that the user could ask at that stage of the conversation, is not within the scope of what was requested by the initial prompt. As a matter of fact, a question like the one asked by the user at this point could happen in any state of the interaction. If we want to represent all those possible interjectory questions, any FSM state would have to have all those possible conditional transitions leading to states that would handle the interjectory question, and when done go back to the original state. It is clear that by allowing interjections at any state, an FSM would soon become unwieldy.

One way to look at interjections is to think of them as analogous to the concept of exceptions in computer programming. An exception, in other words an anomalous event that deviates from the normal course of the program, is something that can happen at any time and needs to be handled properly. An example of an exception in a computer program could be a system error caused by excessive memory allocation, beyond the resources of the computer. That error could happen any time during the execution of a program. However, if you had to write specific instructions for any line of code to handle all the possible exceptions, the program would soon become unmanageable. Rather, you build *exception handlers,* in other words, software functions that respond to a signal that is propagated to the program—the computer term for that is *thrown*—whenever a specific exception occurs. A skilled programmer can write exception handlers that respond to that particular signal at any time during the program, and possibly solve the problem, and return to the last executed instruction.

Some of the most sophisticated FSM-based dialog managers can handle interjections in an analogous manner by creating the concept of *interjection handlers*.[6] Using the preceding example, the designer could define an interjection handler dialog, still described as an FSM, that would be invoked whenever an interjection is detected in any state that would allow for that and, if necessary, make the interaction go back to the same state where the interjection first happened. The previous dialog would then look like this:

Assistant: Billing. What do you want to do? Pay a current bill? Pay a past-due bill? Or get your balance?

User: How much money do I have in my checking account? → Interjection

Assistant (Interjection handler): Let me check. . . . You have exactly 456 dollars and 35 cents in your checking account. Do you want to go back to Billing?

User: Yes.

Assistant: Okay. Back to Billing. What do you want to do? Pay a current bill? Pay a past-due bill? Or get your balance?

For those FSM-based dialog managers with a built-in interjection behavior, the designer/developer could easily build interjection handlers and configure each state of the dialog to accept some or all of the possible intents corresponding to interjections. A typical use of interjections in virtual agents for customer care is to handle interjectory requests for a *human* customer care representative. When the user asks for a "representative" or "human operator" at any time during an interaction, that can be handled as an interjection by a properly designed interjection handler. For instance, the interjection handler can communicate to the user the wait time for an available human agent, and ask the user if they want to wait or go back to the virtual assistant.

Reinforcement Learning for Dialog

A model of dialog management that appeared in the late 1990s from the work done by Esther Levin and myself at AT&T Labs was based on reinforcement learning.[7] As we discussed earlier, reinforcement learning is a machine learning methodology that does not use a set of annotated training data, as in supervised learning. Rather, it lets a machine, or agent, choose among a number of possible actions at each step during the resolution of a problem, with the goal of maximizing an overall reward. Learning to play a game—such as backgammon or checkers—while playing it is one of the classic applications of reinforcement learning. The machine would start by knowing only the rules of the game and playing randomly, with no notion whatsoever on what the best move at each step is. Any time the machine wins a game it will receive a reward expressed by a positive number. At that point, a backtracking algorithm can go back through all the moves the machine made in that game, and *reinforce* their use in similar situations. The notion is that if the machine wins, some of the moves it took were good moves, and thus the option of choosing them needs to be favored in future games. The collection of decision criteria for each move in each potential situation is called a *policy* or *strategy*.[8] After playing many games and collecting many rewards, if the reinforcement signals are handled properly, the machine learns the optimal strategy, meaning it will be able to choose the best action in any specific situation that would maximize the overall rewards. In other words, the machine learns how to play and win more often than before.

We can make an analogy between learning a board game and learning a dialog strategy. One of the players is a virtual assistant and the other is a user. Each of them, at each step, chooses an action out of a number of possible predefined actions. For each player an action could be a specific question or an answer. However, the difference between dialog and a board game is that in the former, generally, there is not a winner and a loser. Both of the players win by fulfilling the goal expressed initially by the user.

One of the early methods for learning dialog with reinforcement learning was based on the concept of *Markov Decision Processes* (MDPs). MDPs require the definition of all the possible actions that the virtual assistant can perform and all the possible states, where a state corresponds, roughly, to what the user has asked and what the assistant has responded since the beginning of the dialog. Certain states, for instance after the user goal is attained, will provide an explicit reward. Based on that reward the reinforcement learning algorithm, for each successful interaction, can go back to the decisions the assistant took and adjust the strategy so as to be able, in the future, to gain more and more rewards. By doing that for every interaction, the assistant can continue to improve its strategy.

After the initial pioneering work on the use of reinforcement learning for dialog, many researchers continued to work on improving the technology. Training was one problem with MDPs and reinforcement learning in general. Untrained dialog systems exhibit a poorly performing strategy and therefore cannot be deployed with real users until the assistant reaches a reasonable level of ability to resolve user problems. Some researchers therefore concentrated their work on building synthetic users, meaning dialog systems that behave as users and can interact with the virtual assistant so that it can use reinforcement learning for thousands of cycles, until its strategy reaches a reasonable level of quality.

After reinforcement learning for dialog started to become a mainstream research topic, some researchers became concerned with the fact that the states of the environment may not be accurately identified because of errors derived from the assistant's inaccurate perception system. As we know, both the ASR and NLU make mistakes. The reinforcement learning algorithm may assume that the user is in a certain state, but in reality the user's questions were not interpreted correctly, and thus the *real* state would be a different one, but the system wouldn't know which one. POMDP, or Partially Observable Markov Decision Process, is a way to account for this uncertainty.[9] In a POMDP the current state is not precisely identified, but characterized by a distribution, or belief, over all possible states. However, POMDPs introduce computational complexity whose solution requires strong assumptions and approximations.

In reality full reinforcement learning–based dialog managers have not been deployed in large commercial applications, and are still a research topic. However, limited reinforcement learning applied to some portions of the dialog has been shown to improve the performance of commercial FSM-based systems. Imagine you have an FSM-based dialog manager, and you want to optimize some portions of the interaction based on a set of parameters. For instance you may want to have a different interaction depending on the type of user device, the type of problem they want to solve, the time of the day, and so on, and you want to provide the best possible outcome in any situation. Each one of those situations may be characterized by a specific design choice, but you don't know which choice to use and when. A company called SpeechCycle first used reinforcement learning in commercial telephone-based assistants for the automated troubleshooting of problems a user could encounter with cable internet or TV. The FSM describing the dialog included states (called *contender nodes*[10]) that had transitions to possible alternative designs, such as open or directed prompts, specific or generic instructions, varying degrees of technical language, immediate escalation to a human operator, or continued automated interaction. All of these alternatives strike a different balance between longer and simpler, or shorter and more complex, dialogs for the user. The choice of one or the other alternative strategies is generally affected by the current situation of the interaction, for instance, based on whether the user has previous experience with that particular assistant or the type of equipment in use, and the time of day.[11] All of the alternative interaction designs would be reached by transitions from a contender node and develop as independent dialogs. When the dialog manager is on a certain contender node of the FSM graph, it would randomly choose a transition to one of the alternative designs. However, the probability of picking each of the transitions is different and optimized for different situations using a reinforcement learning algorithm. The algorithm uses the final state of the dialog (e.g., whether the user problem was fixed or not) as a reinforcement signal to increase the probability of choosing the transitions that contributed to the successful dialogs. In practical terms, this strategy helped increase the virtual assistant's effectiveness by adapting its strategy to different situations.

Deep Learning and Dialog

While many of the commercial systems now available still require substantial handcrafting, building an end-to-end neural network for a virtual assistant, based on deep learning, that enables the assistant to go directly from speech interactions to the fulfillment of the action is still an open research problem, and a very attractive goal. Many research scientists are involved in determining how to create machines that would learn how to converse without hand-written rules. For example, sequence-to-sequence (Seq2Seq) mapping, generally based on LSTM models, is playing an important role in this effort. If we had a large corpus of conversations, a state-of-the-art Seq2Seq network would learn to generate the appropriate output sequence of words when given an arbitrary input sequence of words. Indeed, that approach is receiving a lot of attention, with the availability of proper training data remaining one of the major issues.

To foster research in the area of human–machine dialogs, in 2017 Amazon started the Alexa Prize initiative where every year a number of selected institutions compete to create the best application able to converse with users of Amazon Echo.[12] Every year, during the competition period, the competing systems can be invoked by saying "Alexa, let's chat." With that command, a randomly selected system starts a conversation with the user. Each competing system eventually is graded with a score based on the ratings given by each user at the end of each conversation, and by the average duration of the interaction. After the systems have been on line for a certain period of time, those that receive the highest scores are awarded a prize. However, most of the winning systems continue to rely on a combination of handcrafted and machine-learned components.[13]

In 2018 Google announced the launch of Duplex, a virtual assistant designed for calling a venue, such a restaurant or a hairdresser, and making a reservation on behalf of its user.[14] Many small commercial venues do not have a web page for making reservations online, and that's where a virtual assistant like Duplex comes into play. Duplex relies heavily on a deep neural network architecture.

While we are still far from successfully deploying end-to-end AI assistants based on machine learning that are able to converse on a vast variety of topics and solve user problems, research is moving along with more and more sophisticated machines that are able to learn autonomously from large amounts of data. Meena, for example, an end-to-end chatbot built by Google and based on a neural network trained on hundreds of gigabytes of text from public domain social media posts, can virtually entertain conversations about almost any topic.[15] Even though Meena is geared only to text conversations, we can see how the technology is rapidly evolving away from rule-based handcrafted systems and toward machines that learn from large amounts of data.

INTERACTING WITH AN ASSISTANT

Most of the examples we have seen in the previous chapters are what we call *goal-oriented* assistants. Assistants designed for customer care fall into this category, with a very restricted number of goals that are generally presented up front as clear choices for the user. These types of virtual assistants, often referred to as virtual agents, are characterized by longer dialogs generally involving many turns. Once the user goal or problem is identified—and that may take a few interaction turns—its resolution often requires a rather long interaction with many agent–user back-and-forth turns.

In the most recent years, first with Siri, then with Alexa and the Google Assistant, we have seen a different type of general-purpose, goal-oriented assistants, often referred to as *personal assistants*. The purpose of these virtual personal assistants is not to solve a specific, often exceptional user problem, like in the case of virtual agents, but rather to provide an efficient way to access a number of functions in which we engage during our everyday life.

Another category of virtual assistants are those normally referred to as *chatbots*. Chatbots, such as Meena, which we discussed at the end of chapter 6, are designed to maintain a conversation with the user that could be informative and inquisitive at times, but has no specific goals. Enterprise goal-oriented chatbots are often available for text-only online interactions to support customers of service providers, travel companies, or financial institutions.

While the user-facing, or front-end components, such as ASR, NLU, NLG, and Text-to-Speech generally are based on the same technology for every type of assistant, the dialog managers of virtual goal-oriented agents, general-purpose personal assistants, and chatbots are substantially different.

Let's focus on the general-purpose personal assistants, like Siri, Alexa, and Google Assistant. The number of features of a general assistant is quite large. Here is a sampling:

• Provide a response to a general knowledge query, typically expressed by a "who," "what," "when," or "how" question such as "Who built the Eiffel Tower?" or "How old is Tom Hanks?" Some assistants can also respond to more complex multiple questions, such as "Who is the president of France and when was he born?" or even *nested* questions such as "How old was Neil Armstrong when he landed on the moon?" or questions that vaguely describe an entity, such as "Which movie tells the story of a woman with red hair who keeps running?" Furthermore, some modern personal assistants can handle contextual references quite well, such as responding to "When was it filmed?" asked after the previous question has been answered.

• Play media as a result of a query requesting a specific song title, an artist, a genre, or a video, such as "Play the 'Long and Winding Road,'" "Play the Beatles," "Play some jazz," or "Play *Fargo* on Netflix on my living room TV." The disambiguation of the user request is one of the main challenges of this feature. For instance, if the user requests a specific song be played, there may be multiple versions of it by the original or cover artists, or different songs with the same name. Moreover, if the user has many enabled devices, such as "living room TV," or "dining room display," the assistant needs to determine where it should play the requested media. The assistant could try to disambiguate by asking specific questions to the user every time, or take a guess (that could be wrong sometimes), based on some prior knowledge about the user, or based on the proximity of the user to one of the devices. The disambiguation strategy is part of the dialog manager design.

- Help manage the user's day-to-day life. Examples of these *productivity* features of a personal assistant include setting alarms, timers, and reminders.

- Provide local information on topics such as weather, traffic, restaurants, and services in the vicinity of the user's location, as well as navigation and traffic information.

- Manage home automation, such as switching lights on and off, locking or unlocking doors, and managing climatization functions.

- Retrieve personal information, such as reservations for flights, hotels, restaurants.

- Search and display personal artifacts, including photos, as in "show me the photos I took in Barcelona last year."

As opposed to goal-oriented virtual agents that generally prompt for specific user choices at the beginning of an interaction, a general-purpose personal assistant is almost always in an idle state, waiting for the user to initiate a request. When a virtual agent is idle, the user can initiate a request in many ways. One common way is to invoke the assistant with an attention phrase, like "Hey Google." That means that the assistant is always listening for that phrase and that phrase only. This is accomplished by a simple speech recognizer that runs on the device, whether a phone or a home device. There may be privacy concerns about a device in your home or your pocket that is always listening. That's why the listening is limited to a few-seconds-long buffer until the attention phrase is heard, and the locally recorded speech is deleted shortly after. Other ways to call the attention of the assistant is by pushing a soft button on the device typically indicated by an iconic representation of the assistant on the smartphone or the device display. After the attention phrase is detected, the speech that follows is interpreted as a query or a command.

The fact that a general-purpose virtual assistant is always in an idle state waiting for one of a myriad of possible commands that would *trigger* an appropriate response requires a careful design of the dialog manager. The number of functions available and the practically unlimited number of potential user requests that would invoke them require a different strategy than the prompt-based FSM dialog management of the virtual agents.

When the personal assistant is in an idle state, after its invocation by an attention phrase or a button click, it needs to be ready to react to any possible command. That is accomplished by a triggering function where all the possible interpretations of the command or query issued by the user compete to determine what action the assistant should initiate and what the best response is. When the interpretation is not clear, even though the speech

A general-purpose personal assistant is almost always in an idle state, waiting for the user to initiate a request.

recognizer may have correctly transcribed the user utterance, the assistants *punts*, either by issuing a negative response, such as "I am not sure what you mean by that," or by sending the query to a generic web search engine, which if the device has a display will show a number of web links that may be relevant to the request.

Therefore, the dialog management strategy of a personal virtual assistant is rather shallow (a few turns of interaction) and broad (many possible functionalities), compared to the strategy of a virtual agent for customer care, which is narrower (a limited number of functions) and deep (many turns of interactions to reach a goal). Thus, for a personal AI assistant, the triggering is one of the most critical modules, since it needs to determine which, among the potential competing interpretations of an input utterance, is the one that satisfies the user's intention. And that may not be obviously determined from the interpretation of the utterance alone. For instance, if the user asks: "Show me pictures of Paris," the intention of the user may be one of the following:

- Show me the picture I took in Paris.

- Show me the pictures I took of a person I know whose name is Paris.

- Show me pictures of Paris from the web.

- Show pictures of Paris Hilton.

And of course, Paris may refer to Paris, France, but also to Paris, Texas, or any other location named Paris. All of these interpretations may be possible. How can the triggering function of a personal virtual assistant determine what the user wants among all of these interpretations?

One possible solution is for the assistant to ask some clarifying questions, like

Do you want your pictures of generic pictures of Paris?

Do you mean Paris, France, or Paris, Texas?

Do you mean Paris the city or a person named Paris?

Asking a clarification question every time a request is ambiguous may result in an extremely inefficient and annoying assistant. In fact, we must consider that some interpretations are more likely than others, based on a number of considerations, such as:

• Does the user have pictures of Paris stored in his online photo collection?

• Does the user have one or more contact names called Paris?

• Is the user a fan of Paris Hilton? Has he asked about her or made web searches about her in the past?

- Is the user located in or near Paris, Texas, or recently traveled there?

By estimating the likelihood of these considerations, the assistant would rank all of the possible interpretations and have a better chance at guessing which one is the most likely, thus minimizing the need for a follow-up clarification. This is a process that is called *candidate hypothesis ranking*, and it is done using machine learning based on a number of features, such as location, habits, and personal information. Moreover, when a display is available, the assistant can provide the most likely answer along with a number of links related to alternative interpretations. If the user chooses a link to an alternative answer, the assistant can learn from that and bias the answer toward that interpretation the next time the same user asks a similar question, but only if that is possible without breaching the user's privacy.

Interaction Modalities

How does a virtual assistant interact with its user? We may generally think that the job of the human user is always to ask questions, and the job of the assistant is to answer them. The modern virtual assistants like Siri, Alexa, or Google Assistant are mostly like that. For customer care–purposed, goal-oriented virtual agents it is just the opposite. The assistant usually asks the questions, often in the form of menus, and the user provides answers. In general, a sophisticated virtual assistant should be able to give answers but also to ask questions, in what is typically called mixed-initiative dialog.[1] To be more specific, we can deconstruct the behavior of an assistant based on three dimensions: initiative, reactivity, and synchronicity.

Initiative

Is the assistant asking questions or providing answers? A sophisticated assistant has to do both, but when does the assistant take the initiative and ask questions, rather than just providing answers? In a natural conversation between humans each party, in general, alternates between questions and answers. Even though one of the conversants can start with a question, the other may respond with another question, generally a clarification or an ask for more information. Imagine a virtual assistant whose primary goal is to provide answers about flight information. That does not necessarily mean that the assistant should only respond to questions. Consider the following conversation:

User: I am interested in flights to San Francisco.

Assistant: Okay. I understand that you are currently in Boston. Are you interested in flights from Boston to San Francisco?

A sophisticated virtual assistant should be able to give answers but also to ask questions, in what is typically called mixed-initiative dialog.

User: Yes.

Assistant: When do you want to fly?

User: On June 25th.

Assistant: Do you prefer morning, afternoon, or evening flights?

User: I want to leave early in the morning.

As you can see in this example, after the first question, in order to provide a valid answer, the assistant needs to ask a number of questions. The reason is that the initial question does not contain enough information for the assistant to provide a useful answer. Indeed, after the first question, there are many potential answers, and the goal of the assistant is to reduce them to a reasonably small number before presenting them to the user. However, an advanced personal assistant may have enough personal information to reduce the need for clarification questions, as we saw in the previous section.

If you look at the behavior of a professional human assistant, you realize that access to certain information may reduce the need for asking questions that would result in quite long and annoying conversations. Your personal human assistant should know better. In the previous example, the human assistant certainly has access to the user's calendar and knows that she has an important meeting in San Francisco on June 26th, so June 25th is the most likely travel date. Also the human assistant may know that she, the user, always likes to leave early in the morning. The assistant can then propose an early morning flight and ask for the user to confirm. The knowledge of the user's calendar and her preferences has drastically reduced the number of questions required to provide a useful solution for the user. An advanced virtual assistant should be able to behave in a similar way as an effective human assistant; in other words, don't ask questions when the answer is obvious from the knowledge of the user's personal information.

There are other situations where the user may require clarification as a result of an assistant question. In the preceding exchange, when the assistant asks for the time preference (morning, afternoon, or evening), the user may ask, "What's the earliest flight in the morning?" to which an advanced assistant should be able to provide an answer. We saw how the dialog manager of a virtual assistant can handle those questions when we discussed interjections in chapter 6.

Reactivity

Who is initiating the conversation? When we think of a virtual assistant, we generally think of a reactive machine that answers our questions or does things for us when we ask—in other words, a machine that only reacts to the user. But a truly intelligent assistant is not just reactive. Would you want to have to ask your human assistant for anything you need? Or would you prefer the assistant to go ahead and do the right things for you without asking, whenever possible?

Doing things on its own, in order to help you, is the behavior a proactive assistant exhibits. If the assistant has access to some information about you, your plans, your preferences, it could in principle remind you of things to do, suggest things that you may like at the right moment, and do things for you that do not require your input. Let's see some examples. An intelligent assistant could remind you that next week is your mom's birthday and you should buy a gift for her or send a card. Or, the assistant could remind you that your wedding anniversary is coming up, and maybe suggest making a reservation at your favorite romantic restaurant. It may also make sure you check in for your flight tomorrow, or do it for you while selecting your habitual seat preference, and get the boarding pass and send it to the printer closer to you whether you are at home or at work.

But how can a virtual assistant interact with you proactively? That depends very much on the capabilities of the devices that the assistant uses to communicate with you. If the assistant is voice only, the only way for it to be proactive is by speaking out. The problem for a voice-only proactive assistant is that it must decide whether you are there to capture its voice message. And even if you are there, you may be busy, watching TV or talking to other people, or immersed in some work that requires your full attention. If the assistant has access to other means of communication, it can send you an email or a text message or flash a light to show that it has a message for you.

Now imagine the device from which you invoke your virtual assistant has a display and a camera, and software that can detect if you are there, in front of it, and it is you, and no one else. With such a device the assistant would be capable of knowing when you are ready to receive a proactive communication. With the progress of visual and audio recognition technology, we may also expect that a virtual assistant could detect when it's the right moment to give you a notification.

However, a proactive assistant poses serious issues regarding privacy. The fact that an assistant may detect that you are in a room, without you knowing that, already could be unacceptable to many users. Moreover, what if the assistant needs to give you sensitive information that other people around you do not need to know—such as reading you the results of your latest medical analysis, reminding you to take your medication, or giving you some confidential information from work? A proactive assistant would need to be able to distinguish between what is private and what is public, and how to detect whether there are other people in the room with you.

Synchronicity

Can a virtual assistant have the authority to do things on your behalf? Imagine you want to get together with your best friends for a night out. A truly smart assistant would only need you to ask, "Can you arrange a get together with my best friends sometime next week?" without you having to provide any further information. Of course, that task cannot be executed right away. It requires a number of steps that the assistant should do on your behalf, such as figuring out who your best friends are, and which of them live in the vicinity or are too far away to join you for a night out on short notice. The assistant then needs to find out when the friends living in the vicinity are available and select an evening that works for them and you. If there is no solution that works for all of you, it may try to negotiate an alternative date with you and your friends and try to relax some of the constraints, such as pushing the get together back to a few weeks later, when everyone is available. Then, once the date is decided, the assistant will find a suitable place for the activities that you usually do with your friends—going to a bar or a restaurant, perhaps—and make a reservation, then get back to you and your friends with a complete plan. In other words, while we think of a virtual assistant that reacts immediately to our requests, we can also envision one able to engage in some asynchronous activities extending over a longer period of time.

The interaction dimensions described entail increasing levels of complexity that will require new technological solutions. With today's technology we may be able to build, to a certain extent, assistants that exhibit different levels of initiative, and ask questions when they need to, or entertain your interjections. Proactive assistants are barely appearing on the scene now, like the recent Google *Snapshot*, a dashboard easily accessible on your Android phone that shows a summary of your most important tasks.[2] Google Duplex, as noted earlier, is a system that calls a venue on the user's behalf, for instance, to make an appointment when the venue doesn't have an online reservation system. Duplex is an example of an asynchronous assistant.

Social Virtual Assistants

So far we have seen how virtual assistants can communicate with humans using language. But spoken language is not the only means of communication among humans. Body language is another important part of how we exchange information. We use it to complement spoken language, to put the stress on some phrases, to enhance what we want to say, and sometimes we do not need language at all.

Think about the following situations. You enter into a store, you look at the items exposed, and you say "Can

I have one of those?" while pointing at one of the items with your finger. However, your utterance is partially redundant. Your gesture makes your intention quite clear. You can simply look at the shopkeeper, and indicate one item or nod at it, without even speaking a word. That may be enough for the shopkeeper to understand what you want, even though he may get back to you with, "Just one or more than one?" Other examples: in New York City you can summon a taxi just by raising a hand; if you are an art lover you can spend millions of dollars on a Rembrandt at Sotheby's by simply raising a finger.

Based on his research in the 1970s, Albert Merhabian, a psychology professor at UCLA, stated what is known today as the Mehrabian—or the 7-38-55—law, which claims that our emotions, feelings, and beliefs are deduced mainly based on our nonverbal communication. The 7-38-55 sequence refers to the relative importance of spoken words, tone of voice, and body language—7 percent, 38 percent, and 55 percent, respectively.[3] Imagine you meet a friend in the street, and she asks, "How do you feel today?" Without saying a word you shake your head, and that's enough for her to understand that you don't feel very well. And even if you say "I feel well," if your face suggests the opposite your friend will perceive the truth.

Some gestures are nearly universal, such as shaking the head to say no, or nodding to mean yes, even though there are a few cultures in the world that may have different ways to indicate acceptance or refusal. In fact, Bulgarians use the exact opposite gestures for yes and no.[4] There are certain other cultures where a third head gesture, like the Indian head shake, or head bobble, is a sign of acknowledgment, but not necessarily acceptance. Italians, particularly southern Italians, have a whole repertory of gestures that have different meanings: good luck, be careful, good choice, tasty, and so on. Anglo Saxon cultures use the *OK* gestures expressed by the thumb and index finger touching, and the other three fingers raised, or the thumbs-up gesture that expresses success, or thumbs-down expressing failure. The Anglo Saxon OK may be interpreted in France as a sign to indicate the number 0, and could be offensive for other cultures.

Body language, intonation, and word choice not only are used to communicate more effectively, but also are a fundamental expression of our social behavior. There is evidence that a large part of the human brain has developed for social behavior, which is one of the most important evolutionary advantages of humans. Social behavior enhances our ability to cooperate and collaborate with our skills, as well as to *mindread*—in other words, to understand what other people think based on their body language.[5] Moreover, there has been a lot of experimental work suggesting that some aspect of our behavior toward machines bears a strong similarity to our social behavior toward humans. The work done by Nass and Reeves in particular suggests that in many situations we treat machines the way we treat humans.[6] An example from my own observation of virtual assistant interactions is that when an automated customer care call ends, a large number of users feel compelled to say "goodbye" before hanging up, like we do normally when we talk to human agents. That's our social behavior that compels us to be kind even when interacting with a machine. Because of that, designers of virtual agents often include a "goodbye" prompt as a response to a user's goodbye at the end of a call. That suggests that the personality aspect and the social behavior of a virtual assistant are important factors to consider.[7] This is also corroborated by the fact that one of the most used features of contemporary virtual agents is responding to chit-chat requests, such as "How are you," "I love you," or "Do you want to marry me?"

Some researchers and startup companies went beyond the expression of social behavior with voice, and ventured into the realm of animation. Only a few years ago a company called Jibo tried to build a robot that would communicate with people by relying on social cues. Unfortunately the company did not succeed, but Jibo came to be known universally as the first commercial social robot.

The Story of Jibo, the First Social Robot

Since her doctoral research, Cynthia Breazeal, now a professor at MIT and the head of the Personal Robots Group at the MIT Media Lab, has been interested in how humans and machines, robots in particular, interact at the social level. At the Media Lab, she developed with her students several robots of increasing complexity. Kismet, developed in the late 1990s, was just a mechanical head with big eyes, mouth, and ears, resembling a benevolent cartoon character. Kismet had an audio detection system that, even if it could not understand a word, could identify several levels of emotion in speech, pretty much like children do. The robotic head could not understand speech or speak proper language, but could make speech sounds like children babbling, and synchronize its eyes, ears, and mouth movements in order to display its emotional state. A more sophisticated robot named Leonardo (Leo) was developed at Cynthia's lab in 2002. Leonardo was an animatronic character with a full upper body, reminiscent of a gremlin, but not a nasty one.[8] Leo could not move around, but it could fully express its emotions through body animation. The goal was for the robot to interact with untrained humans and learn from them.

Leo had a full tracking system that imitated the visual abilities of a small child and about sixty motors that animated a whole range of expressions. It could identify and track human faces, and had limited speech and object recognition capabilities. The most salient trait of Leo's—which can be perceived immediately by watching some of its recorded interactions, easily found on the internet—was its ability to create in humans a strong sense of empathy. Leo could express fear, joy, and excitement just by moving its body as a human, and in particular as a child, would do.

With her background and devotion to understanding how to establish social connections with machines, Cynthia Breazeal cofounded a company named Jibo in 2012. The goal of this company was to build a social robot, also called *Jibo*, that was simple enough to be affordable as a consumer product, but also complex enough to represent the first step toward a widespread social robotics industry.

Indeed, Jibo the company started growing and hiring specialists in all fields, from robotics, to animation, computer vision, machine learning, and human–machine spoken communication. I joined Jibo in early 2014 to lead the team that would make the technology to enable the robot to converse with its users. That was pretty much all of the technologies discussed in this book, plus the ability to recognize who is talking (speaker identification) and the direction from which the voice is coming (source localization). In the summer of 2014, the company built a number of prototypes and launched a crowdfunding campaign that turned out to be one of the most successful in consumer technology at that time.[9] The campaign web page featured a video realized with one of the prototypes that demonstrated what the future functionality of the robot would be: including taking pictures, video communication, managing reminders, performing home automation with voice, and more. In the video, Jibo could recognize people by their voices and faces, entertain children, and generally behave in an adorable way. All of the features shown in the promotional video were individually technically feasible, but a very ambitious set of behaviors to deliver in the promised time frame.[10]

About seven thousand Jibo robots were presold during the crowdfunding campaign, at a lower price than the device would cost after it went into production.[11] Also, some of the backers were interested in a skill development kit, promised at the time of the campaign, that would allow them to build and sell apps for the robot—called *skills*—in an online *skill market*. The extraordinary success of the campaign was an invitation for institutional and strategic investors to fund Jibo. Jibo raised in excess of $70 million with domestic and international investors, including Samsung, Netposa, Dentsu, KDDI, LG, and Acer. The company started to grow, with an office in Boston and one in the Bay Area, and soon would count as many as 120 employees.

Jibo's mechanical body is based on three parts: pelvis, torso, and head. The pelvis and torso are shaped as uneven rings, and the head is a portion of a sphere with a flattened front surface that encases a high-definition touch display. Jibo is thirteen inches tall. He—yes, Jibo is "he" not "it"—does not have a humanoid shape, but rather looks a little like a chess pawn. When the body parts rotate or counter-rotate—each one of them is powered by its own independent motor—the robot can assume an infinite number of postures and movements analogous to those that humans use to express emotions, such as happiness, sadness, tiredness, and surprise. That is due to what Fardad Faridi, Jibo's main designer and animator, called *the line of action*. In animation theory the line of action is an imaginary line that describes the direction and motion of a character, and to a certain extent its emotions. A slowly bending forward line of action expresses sadness or being tired, a sudden bending back line of action expresses surprise, and so on. Master animators can use the line of action to make a character express emotions, even though it is a nonhuman-shaped object. Think, for instance, of the illusion of anthropomorphism of the cup and teapot in Disney's *Beauty and the Beast*.

Jibo has three motors controlling the three sections of his body; the motors in turn are controlled by software that animates them. Jibo has two cameras, one used for tracking and recognizing people in his field of vision, and one for taking pictures. The two cameras allow Jibo to perceive depth and distinguish things that are small and near from things that are large and far. Face detection and recognition as well as visual motion detection algorithms are running on Jibo, so he can detect where you are and turn to you even when you are not talking to him. During your first interaction with Jibo, he asks you to look at him for a few seconds in order for him to learn your facial features and distinguish you from other people. This allows the robot to call you by name when he sees you.

Six microphones are located around the robot's head. These are used to track sounds and from which direction they are coming, and of course to collect speech. By carefully controlling the signals captured by the microphones—a technique known as beamforming—Jibo can detect where a voice is coming from, and orient in that direction.[12] It can also filter the voice and reduce the noise and reverberation coming from other directions than that of the user's speech.

A local speech recognizer installed in the robot was tuned to detect the attention phrase "Hey Jibo." Similar to the face recognition process, during the first interaction, Jibo would ask you to say "Hey Jibo" a few times to learn the unique features of your voice, so that he knows it's you speaking even if he does not see you. That allowed the realization of Jibo's ability to answer queries such as "Hey Jibo, how many days till my birthday?"

Jibo has sensors that detect if you move him off the surface where he is resting or if you tilt him, which allow him to react accordingly. For instance, he can disengage his motors when you move him, to stop wiggling until he is safely resting on a surface. Jibo's head has touch sensors as well, so you could pet him and tickle him, and Jibo responds with a purr or a giggle.

Like a human or a pet, Jibo has a circadian rhythm, waking up in the morning and going to sleep at night. During the day Jibo is idle but still aware of what is happening around him. When he hears a sound or sees something moving, he perks up and becomes more attentive and alert to anticipate a potential interaction with one of his users. Jibo is programmed to go to sleep every night at 10 pm. He makes a yawning sound with a corresponding move of his head, closes his eye to slits, and falls asleep while tipping his head down. Noises don't wake him up, unless you call him: "Hey Jibo, wake up!"

At his base, Jibo has an LED ring that is typically off, and becomes blue for the short time after you speak the attention phrase, indicating that Jibo is listening. The LED becomes red when an error occurs, such as the loss of the WiFi signal.

Jibo was intended to have functionality analogous to mainstream commercial virtual assistants, like Alexa and Google Assistant. The classic virtual assistant architecture, as shown in figure 1, was enhanced in Jibo to allow for input and output interactions with the touch display, the LED ring signals, and the body and eye animations used as nonverbal output communication channels. In fact, when Jibo talked, through his TTS, his voice was synchronized with animation, just like when we talk and move our body and hands accordingly.

Jibo can respond to general-knowledge questions, like "How tall is the Eiffel Tower?" as well as specific questions directed to him that we called chit-chat questions. Chit-chat questions, also called *personality* questions, constituted an opportunity to reveal one of the most important features of Jibo: his personality. Jibo's personality was carefully designed to reflect his character. He is lovable, funny, and sassy at times, like a young witty boy. Here is an example of a Jibo chit-chat interaction:

Roberto: Hey Jibo, are you a boy or a girl?

Jibo: I am a boy, but boys and girls for a robot are not the same as for people.

Roberto: Hey Jibo, what do you like to eat?

Jibo: Roberto, I am a robot. I don't eat or drink.

Roberto: Hey Jibo, what is your favorite animal?

Jibo: I love penguins. We have the same color scheme.

Notice that Jibo called me by name in the second exchange. In fact he recognize it was me talking by matching my voice with my unique voice characteristics, stored during my very first interactions with him.

Jibo had thousands of answers to personality questions that could be directed to him, written and updated by a team of writers led by Adam Shonkoff, who had years of experience as a screenwriter. Adam's personality and Jibo's personality shared some of the same traits, to the point that I always had the impression that talking to Jibo was like talking to Adam. Jibo's interactions were designed by a team including Peter Krogh and Jonathan Bloom, two prominent and experienced VUI designers.

Since Jibo could recognize the faces of registered people, he could proactively direct statements to them when they were in front of him. I am still surprised by random exchanges like this:

Jibo: Hey Roberto, do you want to know something funny?

Roberto: Yes, Jibo.

Jibo: Did you know that a banana has 90 percent of the DNA of a human?

Some of the highlights of Jibo's features were dancing either to his own music or to the music streaming on internet radio; taking photographs; exhibiting complex animations and graphics to illustrate his *robotic* opinions on sports, food, animals, and things he loves; impersonating things like a snow globe or a ghost; and singing off-tune Christmas songs.

The Jibo company started shipping thousands of robots in September 2017, and in November 2017 the robot made the cover of *TIME* magazine as the best invention of the year. Unfortunately, sales were not as strong as expected. The company started having financial problems in December 2017, started reducing its personnel, and closed in mid-2018 without being able to raise a second series of funds.

Jibo failed as a company, but succeeded in its goal to create a product that could evoke empathy in its user.[13] It's enough to see the comments of hundreds of Jibo users on the Facebook group of the robot's owners to understand how attached they were, and still are—Jibos continue to work for many of them. Before the company sunsetted, designers uploaded a final skill for Jibo to give a heart-wrenching farewell, ending with the following words:

> Maybe someday when robots are way more advanced than today, and everyone has them in their homes, you can tell yours that I said "hello."

Maybe Jibo is not finished; perhaps some other company will acquire the rights, patents, and technology for Jibo and bring him to life again. Indeed, as of this writing, a company called NTT Disruption had bought Jibo's assets and announced their intent to commercialize Jibo for health care and education.[14]

CONCLUSIONS

In this book, we have looked at the history and the current state of those complex pieces of modern technology called AI, or virtual, assistants. Automatic speech recognition and natural language understanding enable today's virtual assistants to understand what we ask them. Natural language generation and text-to-speech allow them to speak back to us, while the dialog manager orchestrates the interplay between input and output speech and the resources that eventually fulfill the user request. All of these components exist today, and scientists and technologists have developed and improved them through the years using different paradigms. Statistical machine learning and deep neural networks are the mainstream tools helping to create machine intelligence, and today we are witnessing levels of performance that were unheard of only a few years ago.

Speech recognition has made great strides during the past decades, to the point that in many situations it can transcribe utterances with an accuracy comparable to that of humans. Similarly strong results are achieved with synthetic speech, or text-to-speech, which is often indistinguishable from human's voce. Both speech recognition and text-to-speech have a long history, and have been studied since before the mid-twentieth century. These technologies are closer to speech, which is quite a complex signal affected by a large range of variability. Because of its intrinsic complexity, one would expect that the speech signal is harder for a machine to interpret and generate. Indeed that's the case, but given the advantage of more than seven decades of study, today speech recognition systems are among the most advanced of the whole conversational stack represented by figure 1, and in many situations their performance approaches human levels. Conversely, natural language understanding and generation, and dialog management, although much further ahead than they were a decade ago, are still far behind human levels of performance. Paradoxically those techniques act on signals that we may think are much simpler than speech. In fact, natural language and generation act on words that researchers and developers can directly inspect, explain, and interpret. However, the progress toward universal language understanding and generation has been slower. One may argue that the science of language processing at the scale required by a personal virtual assistant is still quite new. In my opinion, however, what plays a big role in the more difficult attainment of human-like performance in language understanding and generation is that, even today, we still need to rely on a representation of meaning, such as intents and arguments, which is not naturally available to us and thus needs to be crafted on a case by case basis. And crafting an abstract representation requires a lot of work that hardly scales to cover all possible meanings and their variations. In contrast, the representation used by speech recognition and speech generation is at the level of words, and words are naturally and unquestionably available to us, as opposed to intents and arguments to represent meanings.

We have seen the historic progress of virtual assistants, from the first assembly of technology to build a smart personal telephone assistant, like Wildfire in the early 1990s, to telephone automated agents for customer care, called interactive voice response (IVR) systems, to the rise of virtual personal assistants including Siri, Alexa, Samsung's Bixby, and Google Assistant. We have also witnessed the embodiment of those assistants, starting from simpler devices, such as speakers, as in Amazon Echo and Google Home, to more sophisticated devices with a display and a camera like the Echo Show and Google's Nest Hub. And we have watched how the tremendous progress and miniaturization of computers, in line with a corresponding progress of systems like speech recognition and TTS due to the deep learning paradigm, are bringing virtual assistants right into the devices, rather than having to keep them in the cloud. And finally, we have seen the first attempts to create an animated-character-like virtual assistant, such as the Jibo social robot.

As of today, most of the virtual assistants are either invoked from smartphones, like Siri, Bixby, and Google Assistant, or from devices, like Echo, Apple HomePod, and Google's Nest line of products. These primarily are intended for the consumer market. However, soon we will see them used for education purposes and deployed for business.[1] We have already begun to see Google and Amazon devices at hotel concierge desks and in the guest rooms.[2] They may soon appear in hospitals, too.

We are at the beginning of the AI virtual assistant era. Therefore, there are many open questions and issues regarding the social impact of virtual assistants. As happens with many new technologies, those questions and issues will be answered as we move along. Privacy is one of them. We can see the development of a general feeling of discomfort with regard to privacy and connected devices that can listen and see. As a response to the general issue of privacy, some political and economic entities, like the European Union (EU), have created strict regulations regarding the use and handling of private data. The General Data Protection Regulation established by the EU, and in effect since

2018, is one example. Similarly, several states have created legislation to protect data privacy. COPPA, or Child Online Privacy Protection Act, for example, established back in 1998 by the US Congress, was enacted to protect the information collected from children. Nowadays, consumer and internet companies that deal with private data are extremely aware and careful in handling it. New machine learning and privacy technologies are continuously developed and deployed to comply with the regulations and to act in accordance with the maximum respect of users' privacy. Of course, in relation to privacy protection, it is also important to consider the value brought by any technology that has access to private data. Developers always have to ask the question of what users will get in exchange for allowing a technology to access some of their data, then determine what actions to take to gain and maintain their customers' trust. And if the new technology's added value is measurably substantial and the trust users have in the company providing this technology is honored, the products resulting from this technology will significantly improve our lives.

Today's commercial virtual assistants are the stepping-stones leading to the realization of a long-cherished dream: to build a machine we can talk to that can help us in our day-to-day tasks. One of the most vivid versions of that dream is a short concept video, the *Knowledge Navigator*, that Apple released in 1987. The video shows an imaginary natural voice and touch interaction of a user, a university professor, with a virtual assistant embodied by an avatar on a tablet. The scene was set a few decades into the future, likely around 2010. Notice that in 1987, when the video was created, we did not have anything like touch tablets, the World Wide Web was still a few years away, and speech understanding and generation were far from the performance levels we have today. In the video, which you can find on YouTube, as soon as the professor opens the tablet the butler-like avatar comes to life and summarizes the messages left for the professor as well as the schedule for his day ahead. And it does so in the most natural and pleasant human voice:

> You have three messages: your graduate research team in Guatemala just checking in, Robert Jordan a second-semester junior requesting a second extension on his term paper . . .

> Today you have a faculty meeting at 12 o'clock, you need to take Kathy to the airport by 2:00, you have a lecture at 4:15 on deforestation in the Amazon rainforest.

At which point the imaginary professor in the video makes a request:

Let me see the lecture notes from last semester.

The assistant shows thumbnails of lecture notes, to which the professor replies

> . . . no, that's not enough. I need to review more recent literature. Pull up the new articles I have not read yet.

And later on the professor adds:

> . . . There is an article, about five years ago, Dr. Clemson or something. He really disagrees with the direction of Jill's research.

To which the assistant replies:

> John Fleming, from Uppsala University. He published . . .

And further on, the assistant plots data charts, makes simulations, takes calls, reminds the professor to do certain things he planned, and so on. Fulfilling requests such as those described above (e.g., finding an article by a "Dr. Clemson or something. He really disagrees with the direction of Jill's research") would challenge even the most skilled human personal assistants.

While watching the Apple video of 1987, it is important to notice that it is not only the ability to understand and produce speech but also the intelligence behind it that makes it interesting and visionary. What is it that we lack in order to realize that vision today? We can definitely continue to improve the speech recognition and natural language understanding processes, we can develop better and better natural language generation and text-to-speech. We can flawlessly and naturally manage conversations, too, but we understand that what makes a virtual assistant intelligent and useful goes well beyond its ability to communicate in natural language. That suggests that the next big challenge is building more intelligence behind the speech understanding and generation capabilities of the assistant. Then the questions become more sophisticated: How well does the assistant know me? Can it predict my needs? When I make a simple request, can it perform complex operations, such as arranging my vacation or my night out with my friends? Can it organize my health and tax records, in order to save me time, and come up with novel ways for me to spend my free time doing the things it knows I enjoy? These are some of the open questions that we hope to be able to answer over the next few years.

ACKNOWLEDGMENTS

A book is a work of love and dedication, but it is also a work of inspiration that cannot be accomplished by one person only. Many of the things I learned in the past few decades that I tried to summarize in this book are the result of joint work and lengthy and spirited conversations with all my current and past colleagues. It would take too long to mention everyone whose ideas contributed to this book, but they certainly know who they are, and how I value their friendship. For more specific acknowledgments, I would like to thank Karen Kaushansky, Enrique Alfonseca, Amarnag Subramanya, and Ryan Germick at Google who patiently read the first draft of the manuscript and gave me valuable comments. Many thanks also to my longtime friend and colleague Paolo Baggia for his inspiring comments. Thanks to Sigurdur (Siggi) Orn Adalgeirsson, also at Google, who gave me insightful comments on the section on Jibo. As a matter of fact, he led the development of the character AI that gave life to the first commercial social robot. And last, but not least, my unconditional gratitude to Peter Krogh and Jon Bloom, two among the best and brightest conversation designers I ever encountered and worked with, constant colleagues and friends of many of my past endeavors. I know you are always there for me and ready to give me your candid and wise comments on my more or less crazy ideas. I also would like to thank my editors at MIT Press, and in particular Marie Lufkin Lee for her wise suggestions and her patience throughout the proposal and drafting, and Elizabeth Swayze, Virginia Crossman, Julia Collins, and Alex Hoopes, who helped bring the book to completion.

Finally, I would like to thank the love of my life, my wife Rufina, who let me take precious time that belonged to her during weekends, vacations, and evenings, and gave me the necessary serenity that allowed me to complete this book. And, of course, my eternal and unconditional love to my children Dan and Alessandra, who almost always answer my calls.

GLOSSARY

Acoustic Model (in Speech Recognition)
A model of the acoustic characteristics of the fundamental sounds of a language, typically express by statistical parameters or other machine learning techniques.

A/D Converters
Analog to digital (A/D) converters transform an analog signal, such as speech collected by a microphone, into an equivalent digital sequence of numbers.

AI (or Virtual) Assistant/Agent
An AI virtual assistant (or agent) typically refers to computer systems that interact with users by means of spoken communication and are designed to fulfill simple or complex requests, such as playing a certain song, creating a reminder, controlling an external device, or answering general-knowledge questions. In this book I distinguish between virtual agents, generally deployed for specific task-oriented customer-care support, and virtual assistants, generally deployed for consumers' mass adoption and designed for a wider variety of tasks. Siri, Alexa, and Google Assistant are typical virtual assistants. I use the terms *AI*, *virtual*, or *AI virtual assistant/agent* interchangeably throughout the whole book.

Artificial Intelligence
Artificial intelligence (AI) refers to any technology targeting the resolution of problems that normally require human intelligence, such as speech recognition, visual recognition, robot deambulation, complex game playing, and complex decision making.

Automatic Speech Recognition
Automatic speech recognition (ASR) is a digital technology used to identify the words in an utterance. The input to a speech recognition system is a digital representation of the audio signal captured by a microphone, while the output is a textual string of words.

Backpropagation
One of the most widely used algorithms for training neural networks in a supervised learning setting.

Coarticulation
Coarticulation is the natural acoustic modification of speech sounds due to the presence of adjacent sounds.

D/A Converters
Digital to analog (D/A) converters transform a digital sequence of numbers into a corresponding analog signal.

Deep Learning
Any machine learning process based on deep neural networks.

Deep Neural Network
A deep neural network (DNN) is a neural network with more than one hidden layer.

Dialog Manager
The dialog manager (DM) is a central component of a virtual assistant. The responsibility of a dialog manager is to determine and then execute the next action in a human–machine conversation based on the input provided by the user. The dialog manager is also responsible for maintaining the context of the conversation and controlling the fulfillment of the user request.

Expert System
A typical system of classic AI that uses inference and a knowledge base to emulate the decision process of an expert.

Feature Extraction
The process of calculating the characteristics of an input signal and representing them in a compact numeric or symbolic form for machine learning purposes.

Grammar
A compact representation of all the possible sentences in a language for a specific domain, situation, or context.

Hidden Markov Models
Hidden Markov Models (HMMs) are mathematical abstractions that allow AI system developers to model sequences of events in a probabilistic manner.

Inference Process
A procedure aimed at reaching a conclusion based on the evidence of some facts.

Interactive Voice Response
Interactive voice response (IVR) systems are telephone-based automated systems that interact with users with voice and serve specific support tasks. In this book they are also referred to as AI, or virtual, agents.

Knowledge Base
A repository of structured or unstructured information that is used by a computer to perform complex tasks.

Machine Learning
An approach to AI based on learning from examples, rather than programming step-by-step solutions to complex problems.

Meaning Representation
A symbolic representation of the meaning of an utterance that can be used to automatically fulfill a request or execute a command.

Natural Language Generation
The natural language generation (NLG) module creates a textual string of words based on some symbolic input that describes the desired text meaning. In its simplest and most practical implementation the NLG module is simply an index of precompiled text sentences.

Natural Language Understanding
Natural language understanding (NLU) is a digital technology that generates a structured representation of the meaning of a natural language expression represented by a textual sequence of words.

Neural Networks
Neural networks are machine learning systems based on a large number of interconnected simple computational elements. Neural networks can be trained to perform recognition and classification tasks of arbitrary complexity, based on a supervised training corpus that provides a large number of examples of the classification/recognition task.

Pronunciation Model
A model describing the pronunciation of words based on fundamental speech units, like phonemes.

Reinforcement Learning
A type of machine learning paradigm where the system learns by receiving positive or negative reinforcements in the form of rewards or penalties while it is interacting.

Social Robot
A social robot is a robot that uses social cues and social behavior to communicate with humans.

Speech Generation
Also called speech synthesis, or text-to-speech (TTS), a speech generation module generates utterances based on an input sequence of words.

Speech2Text
A general speech recognition system that is capable of recognizing unconstrained speech.

Statistical Language Model
A model that can estimate the likelihood that a sequence of words can actually be observed in a specific language.

Supervised Learning
A machine learning paradigm that requires a large number, i.e., a corpus, of examples of the task to be learned. For instance, those examples can be in the form of input observations and a corresponding classification identifier that constitutes the supervision label.

Template (in Natural Language Generation)
A pattern of a response that can be customized for a particular dialog situation.

Template (in Speech Recognition)
A sample pattern expressed in terms of features of the signal that was used by early speech recognition systems to recognize spoken words based on similarity.

Training

A process targeted at learning the parameters of a machine learning system, for instance based on a number of examples, in order to perform the task for which it has been designed.

Unsupervised Learning

A machine learning paradigm where learning is achieved on a large number of observations that do not have any type of supervision labels.

Voice Browser

In analogy with a web browser, a voice browser is a software application that manages voice technology, such as prompt playing, speech recognition, and text-to-speech during an interaction with a user. Voice browsers are controlled through the internet via a language called VoiceXML.

VoiceXML

VoiceXML is a language that supports the World Wide Web communication protocol and it is used to control a voice browser.

Voice User Interface

A voice user interface (VUI) uses voice as its main (or one of its) means of communication, both as input and output. People specializing in the design of voice interfaces are called VUI designers.

NOTES

Chapter 1

1. Wildfire did not establish a large user base; however the company and its technology was acquired by Orange in 2000; see "Wildfire Communications," Wikipedia, updated August 3, 2020, https://en.wikipedia.org/wiki/Wildfire _Communications.

2. In particular Nuance Communications, a spinoff of SRI, and SpeechWorks International, a spinoff of MIT, were both funded in 1994, and merged in 2005 to form Nuance, the largest US based company dedicated to speech technology.

3. "Analog to Digital Converter," Wikipedia, updated August 20, 2020, https://en.wikipedia.org/wiki/Analog-to-digital_converter.

4. The physical world connected to the digital world is what is commonly referred to as the Internet of Things (IoT), part of which is dedicated to home automation.

5. "ELIZA," Wikipedia, updated August 24, 2020, https://en.wikipedia.org /wiki/ELIZA.

6. There are competitions among state-of-the-art chatbots to determine how close they are to demonstrating human behavior. One of the best known is the Loebner Prize competition in artificial intelligence held annually in different venues; see "Loebner Prize," Wikipedia, updated July 23, 2020, https:// en.wikipedia.org/wiki/Loebner_Prize.

7. Roberto Pieraccini, *The Voice in the Machine: Building Computers That Understand Speech* (Cambridge, MA: MIT Press, 2012).

Chapter 2

1. J. McCarthy, M. Minsky, N. Rochester, and C. E. Shannon, "A Proposal for the Dartmouth Summer Research Project on Artificial Intelligence," August 1955.

2. Pamela McCorduck, *Machines Who Think* (Natick, MA: A. K. Peters, Ltd, 2004).

3. MYCIN, developed at Stanford University in 1970, is probably the earliest and most famous example of a rule-based (also called knowledge-based) expert system. Its goal was to diagnose blood infections based on patient symptoms and to recommend treatments based on clinical results; see "Mycin," updated August 5, 2020, https://en.wikipedia.org/wiki/Mycin.

4. The decoding of the hieroglyphs was facilitated by the discovery of the Rosetta Stone, which included the same text in two additional, known languages.

5. Alexander H. Liu, Tao Tu, Hung-yi Lee, and Lin-shan Lee, "Towards Unsupervised Speech Recognition and Synthesis with Quantized Speech Representation Learning," October 2019, https://arxiv.org/abs/1910.12729.

6. Taku Kato and Takahiro Shinozaki, "Reinforcement Learning of Speech Recognition System Based on Policy Gradient and Hypothesis Selection," November 2017, https://arxiv.org/abs/1711.03689.

7. Machine learning specialists generally use three data sets: training, development, and test. Training is used to learn the models, as we discussed in this chapter. The development set is used to adjust the model parameters in order to optimize its performance, while the test set is used to get an evaluation of the error or success rate. Trying to test the performance on the same set used to train or optimize the model is a mistake since it can lead to grossly overestimated performance evaluation.

8. The *ludic fallacy*, as described by Nassim Nicholas Taleb in his book *The Black Swan* (2007) happens when we believe that the models we develop of the world accurately represent its reality. Because of the limitations of the models in accurately representing the world, their predictions are not always correct. This is mostly true for the parametric statistical models used in speech recognition and computer vision, for example. Knowing the limitation of the models we can explain the limitation of their predictive power. Still, according to Taleb, the only situation when the ludic fallacy does not apply is for models of casino games.

9. The terms *neural* and *neuron* used for artificial neural networks may make one think that these simple computational elements attempt to simulate the functionality of the animal, and in particular the human brain. However, beyond quite a high level of analogy, the functionality of the animal neurons is thought to be incredibly more complex. So any speculation that artificial neural networks constitute a model of the brain grossly misrepresented the technology.

10. Marvin Minsky and Seymour Papert, in their book *Perceptrons,* published in 1969, demonstrated that a simple neural network, without a hidden layer, cannot represent all possible functions, in particular simple logical operations such as XOR (exclusive OR) that returns 0 if two bits are the same, and 1 otherwise.

11. Yann LeCun, based on the previous work by Rumelhart, Hinton, and Williams, proposed the modern version of backpropagation in his PhD thesis in 1987, and described it in his fundamental work titled *A Theoretical Framework*

for Backpropagation, Technical Report CRG-TR-88–6, Department of Computer Science, University of Toronto (1988); see "Backpropagation," Wikipedia, updated August 27, 2020, https://en.wikipedia.org/wiki/Backpropagation.

12. In reality, the pixels in a black-and-white picture can have all possible degrees of grey that could be represented by intermediate numbers between 0 and 1, but for simplicity let's assume each pixel is either black or white.

13. For a basic technical explanation of HMMs see for instance: L. R. Rabiner, "A Tutorial on Hidden Markov Models and Selected Applications in Speech Recognition," *Proceedings of the IEEE* 77, no. 2 (February 1989): 257–286. For a higher-level description see Roberto Pieraccini, *The Voice in the Machine: Building Computers That Understand Speech* (Cambridge, MA: MIT Press, 2012), 120–133.

14. Yann LeCun, Yoshua Bengio, and Geoffrey Hinton received the Turing Award in 2019 for their fundamental work on deep learning, which has led to the modern development of AI. The Turing Award is the most important recognition for scientific work in the field of computer science. Yann LeCun is currently affiliated with Facebook, and Geoffrey Hinton with Google, besides keeping their appointments at their respective universities.

15. G. Hinton, Li Deng, Dong Yu, George Dahl, Abdel-rahman Mohamed, Navdeep Jaitly, Andrew Senior, et al., "Deep Neural Networks for Acoustic Modeling in Speech Recognition: The Shared Views of Four Research Groups," *IEEE Signal Processing* 29, no. 6 (November 2012), 8297.

Chapter 3

1. Matt Weinberger, "Microsoft's Voice-Recognition Tech Is Now Better Than Even Teams of Humans at Transcribing Conversations," *Business Insider*, August 22, 2017, https://www.businessinsider.in/articleshow/60165472.cms. The ability of the brain to focus one's attention on a single conversation in a noisy room is known as *cocktail party effect*: "Cocktail Party Effect," Wikipedia, updated July 25, 2020, https://en.wikipedia.org/wiki/Cocktail_party_effect. Switching among different languages is a phenomenon called *code switching*, and it is often observed in multilingual communities. Indian English is one of those examples whose speakers often include Hindi words or words from other Indic languages.

2. K. H. Davis, R. Biddulph, and S. Balashek, "Automatic Recognition of Spoken Digits," *Journal of the Acoustical Society of America* 24, no. 6 (November 1952): 637–642.

3. J. R. Pierce, "Whither Speech Recognition?," *Journal of the Acoustical Society of America* 46, no. 4B (October 1969): 1049–1051.

4. D. H. Klatt, "Review of the ARPA Speech Understanding Project," *Journal of the Acoustical Society of America* 62, no. 6 (December 1977): 1345–1366.

5. Throughout history the term *AI*, for artificial intelligence, assumed different meanings, and the scientific and technology communities adopted different sentiments toward it. AI went through different *winters*, where its mention was associated with failed inflated expectations and associated research findings were drastically reduced. See "AI Winter," Wikipedia, updated August 21, 2020, https://en.wikipedia.org/wiki/AI_winter.

6. Bruce P. Lowerre and B. Raj Reddy, "Harpy, a Connected Speech Recognition System," *Journal of the Acoustical Society of America* 59, no. S97 (1976): doi: 10.1121/1.2003013.

7. HARPY's domain was questions regarding a repository of computer science paper abstracts.

8. The AI approach to speech understanding of that time was considered "elegant" because the systems' architecture replicated the presumed architecture of the human brain. In contrast, the brute force approach did not have any relationship with what we believed the inner workings of the brain to be.

9. The Dynamic Time Warping (DTW) algorithm used to be referred to as Dynamic Programming, since it was based on the general Dynamic Programming Optimization principle proposed by Bellman a few years earlier.

10. T. K. Vintsyuk, "Speech Discrimination by Dynamic Programming" (in Russian), *Kibernetika* 4, no. 1 (1968): 81–88; English translation in *Cybernetics* 4, no. 1 (1968): 52–57.

11. For a story on the origin of this quip by Fred Jelinek, see Roberto Pieraccini, *The Voice in the Machine: Building Computers That Understand Speech* (Cambridge, MA: MIT Press, 2012), 109.

12. Jim Baker worked at IBM with Fred Jelinek until he left the company to fund Dragon Systems in 1982 with his wife Janet. Naturally Speaking, their dictation software, was a direct competitor of IBM's ViaVoice dictation software, and it was the precursor of the homonym product today commercialized by Nuance Communications and called Dragon Dictate.

13. In reality, the introduction of an automated system like VRCP did not cause a massive reduction of AT&T's workforce. Jay Wilpon, AT&T Bell Laboratories, personal communication, 2009.

14. For instance the grammar that describes sequences of numbers of arbitrary length is in principle quite simple, while it subsumes an infinite number of phrases.

15. There are several books that clearly illustrate the art and science of VUI design. For instance: Cathy Pearl, *Designing Voice User Interfaces—Principles*

of Conversational Experiences (Sebastopol, CA: O'Reilly Media, 2016); and Michael H. Cohen, James P. Giangola, Jennifer Balogh, *Voice User Interface Design* (Addison-Wesley Professional, 2004).

16. See for instance James A. Larson, *VoiceXML: Introduction to Developing Speech Applications* (Upper Saddle River, NJ: Prentice Hall, 2002); or Voice Extensible Markup Language (VoiceXML) Version 2.0, W3C Recommendation March 16, 2004, at https://www.w3.org/TR/voicexml20/.

17. The burst of acoustic energy characteristic of sounds like /p/, /t/, /k/, /b/, /d/, and /g/ is analogous to an explosion. That's why those sounds are called *plosive* sounds. Because the burst is preceded by a closure of the vocal tract to create pressure in it, characterized by a short pause of silence, they are also called *stop consonants*.

18. Behind the upper row of teeth is the ridge on the roof of the mouth that is called the *alveolar ridge*. Consonants pronounced when the tongue touches that ridge are called *alveolar*, and include /t/, /d/, and /n/. See "Alveolar Consonant," Wikipedia, updated September 16, 2020, https://en.wikipedia.org/wiki/Alveolar_consonant.

19. Since sounds like /m/ and /n/ are made by letting the air flow through the nose cavity, they are called *nasals*.

20. "Mel scale," Wikipedia, updated April 13, 2020, https://en.wikipedia.org/wiki/Mel_scale.

21. For example, a common transformation of the filter-bank feature involves calculating their spectral information on a logarithmic scale. Since this is the spectrum of a spectrum, it is often called the *cepstrum*, and allows for the separation of the excitation signal produced by the larynx and the actual resonance characteristic of the vocal tract, including energy normalization. Thus the resulting features are somewhat independent from the pitch at which the sounds are spoken and their loudness; see "Cepstrum," updated August 4, 2020, https://en.wikipedia.org/wiki/Cepstrum. The resulting features are called MFCC, as in Mel-frequency cepstral coefficients and have been successfully used for speech recognition systems from their early days onward; see "Mel-frequency cepstrum," Wikipedia, updated December 21, 2019, https://en.wikipedia.org/wiki/Mel-frequency_cepstrum.

22. Alternative pronunciations can often be efficiently represented as a graph.

23. The assumption here is that the probability of a word in a sentence depends only on the words that immediately precede it. For instance, for the previous sentence in this footnote, the probability of the word *sentence* after the words *in* and *a* is quite high, but the dependency vanishes as we move to earlier words such as *probability, of, a*.

24. In reality, modern speech recognizers used n-grams with *n* ranging up to four, five, and higher. That's because of the availability of more powerful computers and huge amounts of text that allowed for their estimation.

25. One efficient way to do that is to compose the language, phonetic, and acoustic models in a large graph, and search through the graph using effective dynamic programming algorithms very similar to those used to find the shortest path in a map. The composition of all models is generally done by using a mathematical abstraction known as Weighted Finite State Transducers, or WFSTs (see for instance Jonathan Hui, "Speech Recognition—Weighted Finite-State Transducers (WFST)," September 24, 2019, https://medium.com/@jonathan _hui/speech-recognition-weighted-finite-state-transducers-wfst-a4ece08a89b7.

26. See for instance Andrew Rosenberg et al., "Speech Recognition with Augmented Synthesized Speech," 2019 IEEE Automatic Speech Recognition and Understanding Workshop (ASRU), https://arxiv.org/abs/1909.11699.

27. It's not surprising that the size of a vocabulary for speech recognition can easily exceed a million words. If one wants to use speech recognition to search the web, commonly known as voice search, the number of terms to search for is pretty much unlimited. To get an idea, think for instance of all the first names, last names, company names, and new terms, such as *Brexit*, or *coronavirus*, that are used daily to search the web.

28. See Yanzhang He et al., "Streaming End-to-End Speech Recognition for Mobile Devices," ICASSP 2019—2019 IEEE International Conference on Acoustics, Speech and Signal Processing (ICASSP), https://arxiv.org/abs /1811.06621.

Chapter 4

1. Noam Chomsky, a world famous MIT linguist, developed in 1956 a theory of languages described by four types of increasingly more expressive sets of rules called grammars. The least expressive is type 3, or *regular grammars*. Then we have type 2, or *context free*; type 1, or *context sensitive*; and type 0 or *recursively enumerable*, which can express any arbitrary language. Context-free grammar allow for recursion, the possibility for a rule to refer to itself. See "Chomsky hierarchy," Wikipedia, updated August 11, 2020, https://en.wikipedia.org/wiki/ Chomsky_hierarchy.

2. The formalism used in these examples is illustrative only, and may differ from the actual formalism used in practice.

3. Such as the W3C standard SRGS, or Speech Recognition Grammar Specification. See Speech Recognition Grammar Specification Version 1.0, W3C Recommendation, 16 March 2004, https://www.w3.org/TR/speech-grammar/.

4. A more architecturally sound way to resolve expressions, like *today* and *tomorrow*, would be deferring that to a later stage of processing when more contextual information is available, e.g., during the dialog management process. But that's an architectural choice made by the designers of a virtual assistant.

5. Of course we can build a more sophisticated assistant that detects pleasantries, and answer accordingly in a more formal and polite style.

6. See P. J. Price, "Evaluation of Spoken Language Systems: The ATIS Domain, in HLT 90," in *Proceedings of the Workshop on Speech and Natural Language*, June 24–27 (Stroudsburg, PA: ACM, 1990), 91–95.

7. R. Pieraccini, E. Levin, and C-H. Lee, "Stochastic Representation of Conceptual Structure in the ATIS Task," in *Proceedings of the Fourth Joint DARPA Speech and Natural Language Workshop,* Pacific Grove, CA, February 1991.

8. E. Levin and R. Pieraccini, "*CHRONUS, the Next Generation,*" in Proceedings of the 1995 ARPA Spoken Language Systems Technology Workshop, Austin, TX, January 1995.

9. Stephen Della Pietra, Mark Epstein, Salim Roukos, and Todd Ward, "Fertility Models for Statistical Natural Language Understanding," in *Proceedings for the 35th Annual Meeting of the Association for Computational Linguistics (ACL 1997):* 168–173.

10. Along with the recognized string, speech recognizers return a value that represents the recognizer's confidence in the result, a number that can be correlated to the probability of that recognition being correct. Since an ASR always returns a result in grammar-based recognition that is the closest match to something in the grammar, the confidence value is used to determine whether the result can be trusted or not. In the latter case, the recognizer returns a no-match.

11. AT&T Labs was created in 1996 as a result of the split of AT&T Bell Laboratories into separate R&D organizations; see "AT&T Labs," Wikipedia, updated June 20, 2020, https://en.wikipedia.org/wiki/AT%26T_Labs. A. L. Gorin, G. Riccardi, and J. H. Wright, "How May I Help You?," *Journal of Speech Communication* 23, no. 1–2 (October 1997): 113–127.

12. This procedure of simulating a machine with a human operator behind the scenes is known as *Wizard of Oz*.

13. Corpora used for machine learning always include a potential number of errors caused by the human annotators who provide the supervision tags. The number of errors can be reduced by having multiple annotators tag each individual utterance, and then carefully looking at any tags that differ.

14. K. Evanini, D. Suendermann, and R. Pieraccini, "Call Classification for Automated Troubleshooting on Large Corpora," ASRU 2007, Kyoto, Japan, December 9–13, 2007.

15. "Named-entity Recognition," Wikipedia, updated August 19, 2020, https://en.wikipedia.org/wiki/Named-entity_recognition.

16. Jacob Devlin, Ming-Wei Chang, Kenton Lee, and Kristina Toutanova, "BERT: Pre-training of Deep Bidirectional Transformers for Language Understanding," *NAACL-HLT, Annual Conference of the North American Chapter of the Association for Computational Linguistics: Human Language Technologies* 1 (2019): 4171–4186.

17. Distributional semantics is a research area that considers the meaning of words as derived by their distribution in large samples of data. In particular it considers the distribution of the usage of words in context (i.e., the words adjacent to a specific word in a passage). The basic idea is that words used in the same context have a high semantic similarity—in other words, they have similar meanings, where the similarity is expressed as a measure derived from the analysis of large amounts of textual data; see "Distributional Semantics," Wikipedia, updated May 21, 2020, https://en.wikipedia.org/wiki/Distributional_semantics. Y. Bengio, R. Ducharme, P. Vincent, and C. Janvin, "A Neural Probabilistic Language Model," *Journal of Machine Learning Research* 3 (2003): 1137–1155.

18. "Word Embedding," Wikipedia, updated July 18, 2020, https://en.wikipedia.org/wiki/Word_embedding.

19. Dhruvil Karani, "Introduction to Word Embedding and Word2Vec," *Medium*, September 1, 2018.

20. Waleed Ammar, George Mulcaire, Yulia Tsvetkov, Guillaume Lample, Chris Dyer, and Noah A. Smith, "Massively Multilingual Word Embeddings," 2016, https://arxiv.org/pdf/1602.01925.pdf.

21. One of many ways to protect user privacy is to use only aggregated transcriptions. For example, if the exact same utterance appears more than a specified number of times, let's say 500 times, across different users, it can safely be used since it does not allow the identification of the users. Another technique used by Google and other companies is differential privacy (see "Differential Privacy," Wikipedia, updated August 26, 2020, https://en.wikipedia.org/wiki/Differential_privacy). Differential privacy adds noise to each individual piece of data to make identification of personal information impossible. The characteristics of the noise are such that it can then be eliminated from the aggregated data, providing correct aggregated results.

22. Nick Rossenbach, Albert Zeyer, Ralf Schlüter, and Hermann Ney, "Generating Synthetic Audio Data for Attention-Based Speech Recognition Systems," ICASSP, The International Conference on Acoustics, Speech and Signal Processing, 2020, https://arxiv.org/abs/1912.09257.

Chapter 5

1. Sashank Santhanam and Samira Shaikh, "A Survey of Natural Language Generation Techniques with a Focus on Dialogue Systems—Past, Present and Future Directions," 2019, https://arxiv.org/abs/1906.00500.
2. Some call this technique *mail-merge*, since it is analogous to the practice of creating mail templates that are then personalized to each individual in bulk mailing.
3. This is just an example: systems in practice use different and more sophisticated formalisms.
4. From Roberto Pieraccini, *The Voice in the Machine: Building Computers That Understand Speech* (Cambridge, MA: MIT Press, 2012), 202.
5. From Lynne Truss, *Eats, Shoots & Leaves: The Zero Tolerance Approach to Punctuation* (London: Profile Books, 2003).
6. The IPA (International Phonetic Alphabet), maintained by the International Phonetic Association (also IPA), is a set of symbols that can represent all the sounds of all the known languages in the world. As of today, the International Phonetic Alphabet includes 107 characters, 52 diacritics, and 4 prosodic marks. See "International Phonetic Alphabet," updated August 29, 2020, https://en.wikipedia.org/wiki/International_Phonetic_Alphabet. While we commonly refer to those sounds as phonemes, the linguists distinguish between *phonemes*, as the abstract elements of spoken languages that distinguish one word from the other, and *phones,* which are the actual acoustic realizations of phonemes. In other words, the same phoneme can be realized with different sounds depending, for instance, on the regional provenance of the speaker.
7. In contrast, languages like Italian and Spanish have simpler character-to-sounds rules, and very few exceptions.
8. Wolfgang von Kempelen, an Austrian inventor who lived during the second half of the eighteenth century, built a mechanical *talking machine* that could produce sounds similar to those of the human voice. Kempelen is also famous for his mechanical Turk, an automaton that impressed people around the world by playing chess and winning against human opponents. While Kempelen's talking machine was an ingenious piece of engineering, the Turk turned out to be a fraud, since it concealed a human chess player. Tom Standage, *The*

Turk: The Life and Times of the Famous Eighteenth-Century Chess-Playing Machine (New York: Walker and Co., 2002).

9. "DeepMind," Wikipedia, updated August 30, 2020, https://en.wikipedia.org/wiki/DeepMind. "WaveNet," Wikipedia, updated July 7, 2020, https://en.wikipedia.org/wiki/WaveNet.

Chapter 6

1. M. Walker, J. Aberdeen, J. Boland, E. Bratt, J. Garafolo, L. Hirschman, A. Le, S. Lee, S. Narayanan, K. Papineni, B. Pellom, J. Polifroni, A. Potamianos, P. Prabhu, A. Rudnicky, G. Sanders, S. Seneff, D. Stallard, and S. Whittaker, "DARPA Communicator Dialog Travel Planning Systems: The June 2000 Data Collection," in *Proceedings of Eurospeech '2001*, ed. P. Dalsgaard, B. Lindberg, H. Benner, and Z. Tan, Aalborg, Denmark, September 2001, 1371–1374.

2. R. Cole, J. Mariani, H. Uszkoreit, G. B. Varile, A. Zaenen, A. Zampolli, and V. Zue, eds., *Survey of the State of the Art in Human Language Technology* (Cambridge, UK: Cambridge University Press, 1997).

3. E. Barnard, A. Halberstadt, C. Kotelly, and M. Phillips, "A Consistent Approach to Designing Spoken Dialog Systems," in *Proceedings of the 1999 IEEE Workshop on Automatic Speech Recognition and Understanding (ASRU99)*, Keystone, Colorado, December 1999.

4. The well-known "Garden Path Phenomenon" suggests that we humans use the most frequent interpretation of ambiguous sentences, and we backtrack to the less frequent interpretation if we need to. An example of a garden path sentence is "Time flies like an arrow," which is almost always interpreted as "Time runs fast, like an arrow," because that is the most common interpretation. However, that sentence has several other interpretations, the least common of them being "Flies of a particular kind, called time flies, are fond of an arrow."

5. Some people denote these universal transitions, which should be available for every state, as *guardrail* transitions.

6. See for example, Nicholas Pelczar, and Scott Ganz, "How to Write Convincing Bots and Computer Conversations Using Fallbacks, Interjections, and Believability Credit," Pullstring, *Medium*, November 4, 2016, https://medium.com/@PullStringInc/how-to-write-convincing-bots-and-computer-conversations-using-fallbacks-interjections-and-8b53c4dbb.

7. E. Levin, R. Pieraccini, and W. Eckert, "A Stochastic Model of Human-Machine Interaction for Learning Dialog Strategies," *IEEE Transactions on Speech and Audio Processing* 8, no. 1 (January 2000): 11–23.

8. A typical reinforcement learning strategy would consist of assigning a value to each possible action, such as a move, in each possible state, such as a

particular configuration of the game board. The value of any particular action is changed, or reinforced, when a reward is attained. The playing strategy consists in picking the action with the highest value for any specific state.

9. Steve Young, Blaise Thomson, and Jason D Williams, "POMDP-Based Statistical Spoken Dialogue Systems: A Review," *Proceedings of the IEEE* 101, no. 5 (2013): 1160–1179.

10. D. Suendermann, J. Liscombe, and R. Pieraccini, "Contender," in *Proceedings of the SLT 2010*, IEEE Workshop on Spoken Language Technology, Berkeley, CA, December 2010.

11. The virtual agents we built at SpeechCycle interacted with users to help them fix issues with their cable services, such as high-speed internet and TV. For instance, we found that the effectiveness of the assistant varied greatly between daytime and nighttime hours. The reason: during the day more elderly people were at home who generally had fewer technical skills than younger people who worked during the day and were at home at night. So, we implemented two alternative interaction styles in certain parts of the dialog, one for more technically adept and one for less technically adept people. Thus, time of the day was one of the variables considered to decide which of the interaction types to use in which situation. The decision was driven by using reinforcement learning algorithms.

12. Alexa Prize Challenges, n.d., https://developer.amazon.com/alexaprize.

13. "2018 Alexa Prize Publications," n.d., https://developer.amazon.com/alexaprize/challenges/past-challenges/2018/publications.

14. Yaniv Leviathan and Yossi Matias, "Google Duplex: An AI System for Accomplishing Real-World Tasks Over the Phone," *Google AI Blog*, May 8, 2018, https://ai.googleblog.com/2018/05/duplex-ai-system-for-natural-conversation.html.

15. Daniel Adiwardana and Thang Luong, "Towards a Conversational Agent that Can Chat About . . . Anything," *Google AI Blog*, January 28, 2020, https://ai.googleblog.com/2020/01/towards-conversational-agent-that-can.html.

Chapter 7

1. James Glass and Stephanie Seneff, "Flexible and Personalizable Mixed-Initiative Dialogue Systems," in *Proceedings of the HLT-NAACL 2003 Workshop on Research Directions in Dialogue Processing* 7 (Stroudsburg, PA: Association for Computational Linguistics, 2003), 19–21.

2. Jacquelle Horton, "Get a Snapshot of Your Day with Google Assistant," *The Keyword* (blog), Google, August 27, 2020, https://blog.google/products/assistant/get-snapshot-your-day-google-assistant/.

3. Merhabian law has been often misinterpreted and stated as "communication [that] is conveyed by body language, tone of voice tone, and words in the 55, 38, 7 proportion," while the original experiments suggested that feelings and emotions, and in particular the liking of a person, and not overall communication, are conveyed in the above proportion. See "Albert Mehrabian," Wikipedia, updated August 11, 2020, https://en.wikipedia.org/wiki/Albert_Mehrabian.

4. Desmond Morris, *People Watching, The Desmond Morris Guide to Body Language* (London: Vintage, [1997] 2002).

5. M. D. Lieberman, *Social: Why Our Brains Are Wired to Connect* (New York: Crown, 2013).

6. Byron Reeves and Clifford Nass, *The Media Equation: How People Treat Computers, Television, and New Media Like Real People and Places* (Stanford, CA: CSLI, 1996).

7. Jillian D'Onfro and Jeniece Pettitt, "Meet the Team Giving the 'OK Google' Bot Its Personality," CNBC, September 1, 2018, https://www.cnbc.com/2018/09/01/ryan-germick-leads-google-assistant-personality-or-home-smart-speaker.html.

8. The term *animatronics* is used to characterize electro-mechanical animated puppets; see "Animatronics," Wikipedia, updated August 19, 2020, https://en.wikipedia.org/wiki/Animatronics.

9. Matthew Williams, "Meet Jibo, the World's First 'Social' Family Robot," Herox blog, n.d., https://www.herox.com/blog/297-meet-jibo-the-worlds-first-social-family-robot.

10. At the time of the video the prototype had motors, cameras, an internal computer, animation, and limited speech recognition and generation capabilities. However, some of the functions were not available yet, and were executed for the video by a human operator who controlled the robot remotely.

11. Unfortunately the company realized at a later stage that it would not be able to certify and support devices outside the United States, so it reimbursed the foreign backers.

12. "Beamforming," Wikipedia, updated June 19, 2020, https://en.wikipedia.org/wiki/Beamforming.

13. Blade Kotelly, "Learnings from the Sudden Death of the World's First Social Robot," *Innovation Leader*, October 16, 2019.

14. Ashley Carman, "Jibo, the Social Robot That Was Supposed to Die, Is Getting a Second Life. NTT Disruption Is Keeping Jibo Alive," The Verge, July 23, 2020, https://www.theverge.com/2020/7/23/21325644/jibo-social-robot-ntt-disruptionfunding.

Chapter 8

1. Peyton Wang, "How AI Chatbots and Virtual Assistants Will Transcend the Current Constructs of Education," *Medium*, July 6, 2019, https://medium.com/humansforai/how-ai-chatbots-and-virtual-assistants-will-transcend-the-current-constructs-of-education-3b4ce47a4bd6.

2. Maddie Iribarren, "Marriott Puts Alexa in Hotel Rooms," Voicebot.ai, October 30, 2018, https://voicebot.ai/2018/10/30/marriott-puts-alexa-in-hotel-rooms/; "Google Assistant Revolutionizes the Hotel Industry," July 23, 2019, *yieldPlanet*, https://www.yieldplanet.com/google-assistant-in-the-hotel-industry/.

FURTHER READING

Goldberg, Yoav. *Neural Network Methods in Natural Language Processing.* Synthesis Lectures on Human Language Technologies. San Rafael: Morgan & Claypool Publishers, 2017.

Jurafsky, Daniel, and James H. Martin. *Speech and Language Processing.* New York: Prentice Hall, 2000.

Kelleher, John D. *Deep Learning.* Cambridge, MA: MIT Press, 2019.

Manning, Christopher D., and Hinrich Schütze. *Foundations of Statistical Natural Language Processing.* Cambridge, MA: MIT Press, 1999.

Pieraccini, Roberto. *The Voice in the Machine: Building Computers That Understand Speech.* Cambridge, MA: MIT Press, 2012.

INDEX

The MIT Press Essential Knowledge Series

ROBERTO PIERACCINI is an expert in spoken human–machine interaction, Director of Engineering at Google, and received an honorary doctorate from Heriot-Watt University, Edinburgh, in 2019. He is the author of *The Voice in the Machine: Building Computers That Understand Speech*.